P9-CAO-203

Bell   DT
                                          92
Egypt, from Alexander the Great B4.6
to the Arab conquest   1977

                        415910
        ALUMNI MEMORIAL LIBRARY
              Creighton University
            Omaha, Nebraska 68178

                                    DEMCO

EGYPT
FROM ALEXANDER THE GREAT
TO THE ARAB CONQUEST

DATE DUE

~~JUL 22 76~~	~~ILL Oakdale~~		
~~JUL 22 76~~	~~Pol. 2 months~~		
~~MR 01 '81~~			
	~~1D 30 87~~		
~~MR 16 87~~			
APR 16 1989			
AUG 12 '89			
AUG 12 '89			
SEP 30 '94			
RTD JUN 23 '94			
GAYLORD			PRINTED IN U.S.A.

EGYPT

FROM ALEXANDER THE GREAT
TO THE ARAB CONQUEST

A STUDY IN THE DIFFUSION
AND DECAY OF HELLENISM

Being the
Gregynog Lectures for 1946

by

H. IDRIS BELL

READER IN PAPYROLOGY IN THE
UNIVERSITY OF OXFORD

GREENWOOD PRESS, PUBLISHERS
WESTPORT, CONNECTICUT

DT
92
B4.6
1977

Library of Congress Cataloging in Publication Data

Bell, Harold Idris, Sir, 1879-
    Egypt, from Alexander the Great to the Arab conquest.

    Reprint of the 1948 ed. published by Clarendon Press,
Oxford, which was issued as the Gregynog lectures, 1946.
    Bibliography: p.
    Includes index.
    1. Egypt--History--Greco-Roman period, 332 B.C.-640
A.D. I. Title. II. Series: Gregynog lectures ;
1946.
DT92.B46 1977   932'.02   77-8057
ISBN 0-8371-9093-2

All rights reserved

Originally published in 1948 by Oxford at the Clarendon Press

This reprint has been authorized by the Clarendon Press Oxford

Reprinted in 1977 by Greenwood Press, Inc.

Library of Congress catalog card number   77-8057

ISBN 0-8371-9093-2

Printed in the United States of America

PREFACE

As indicated by the title-page, this volume contains the Gregynog Lectures, delivered, under the foundation of the Misses Davies, Gregynog, in the University College of Wales, Aberystwyth, in November 1946. It is one of the conditions of the foundation that lectures should eventually be published. In preparing the present series for publication I have turned the lectures into chapters and have taken the opportunity not merely to revise but somewhat to expand them, in order to make them a less inadequate treatment of their wide theme than was possible in lectures intended to occupy about an hour in delivery. Otherwise they are printed as read.

The lectures were designed for an audience made up of members of the College staff, of students, and of the general public, but unlikely to contain more than one or two, if any, possessing a specialized knowledge of papyrology. Hence, as my evidence was drawn mainly from the papyri, I thought it advisable to begin with an account of these documents and of the science of papyrology. In the three remaining chapters it would obviously have been out of the question to attempt a continuous political history of Egypt during the period of nearly a thousand years which separates Alexander's invasion from the Arab conquest, even had the paucity of evidence not made such an undertaking impracticable. What I have aimed at is a summary sketch, as clear and readable as I could make it, and as free from technicalities as possible, of the economic, social, and administrative development, political events being referred to only as far as their bearing on the main subject made this necessary. The underlying theme, which gives unity to

415910

ALUMNI MEMORIAL LIBRARY
Creighton University
Omaha, Nebraska 68178

the whole, is, as suggested by the sub-title, the fortunes of Hellenism in its Egyptian environment, the inter-action of Hellenic and Egyptian characteristics, and the gradual weakening and decay of the Hellenic element.

Though I have written mainly for a non-specialist public, the volume may, I hope, interest specialists also as at least a handy conspectus of its subject. I have therefore added at the end notes on each chapter, citing the evidence for various statements, qualifying some which, in so rapid a survey, had to be expressed rather more dogmatically than the evidence warranted, and, for the benefit of those non-specialist readers who may wish to study the theme more intimately, referring to such books and articles as they would find useful. For the same readers I have added after the notes a bibliography to each chapter, preceded by a more general one to books covering the whole period. These bibliographies are severely selective, and in a work intended primarily for English readers I have cited by preference works available in English, though I have not excluded those in foreign languages when there was no equally useful alternative in our own tongue. The list of papyrus publications, with the standardized methods of reference, included in the Bibliography on Chapter I is, however, reasonably complete, omitting only some quite minor publications. A more comprehensive list, which includes Demotic and Coptic papyri, will be found on pages 5–16 of Peremans' and Vergote's *Papyrologisch Handboek*.

I should like to express my gratitude to Principal Ifor Evans and the authorities of the University College of Wales for affording me the opportunity of a task which has given me great pleasure, to the Delegates of the Clarendon Press for undertaking the publication, to one of them, Mr. C. H. Roberts, for reading the whole work in manuscript and making some very useful suggestions, and to Mr. T. C. Skeat of the British Museum for looking up a few references in works not accessible to me at Aberystwyth.

These days of austerity preclude dedication pages of the old type and I have therefore inserted here a dedication to an old friend.

WILHELM SCHUBART

IN TREUER FREUNDSCHAFT

GEWIDMET

February 1948   H. I. B.

CONTENTS

I
PAPYRI AND THE SCIENCE OF PAPYROLOGY

Egypt has at all periods of its history occupied a somewhat peculiar position among the countries of the
world. Readers of Herodotus will recall the passage in
the second book of his history in which, by way of establishing the truth of his assertion that the Egyptians 'in
most of their manners and customs, exactly reverse the
common practice of mankind',[1] he recounts their many
peculiarities of usage. Some of his statements must be
taken with rather more than a pinch of salt, for though
Herodotus was not a liar, as certain critics, ancient and
modern, have accused him of being, he was not always
as critical as he should have been, and the native guides,
on whom he was doubtless dependent for much of his
information, seem to have enjoyed 'pulling his leg' on
occasion; but the passage illustrates vividly the sense of
strangeness, of something peculiar and unique, which
Herodotus, like other travellers, felt in Egypt.

This uniqueness is due ultimately to geographical and
climatic causes. Modern Egypt extends roughly from
the 35th to the 25th degree of longitude and from the
31st to the 22nd degree of latitude, and embraces within
its frontiers an area of 386,110 square miles, but the
greater part of this territory is uninhabitable desert. The
real Egypt, the Egypt in which human beings can live
and till the earth, occupies but 13,578 square miles, an
area not very much larger than Belgium (11,750 square
miles). This inhabited Egypt may be divided into three
parts. There is, firstly, the Delta, a tract of alluvial soil

very happily called by Herodotus, as by Hecataeus
before him, 'the gift of the river'.[2] It was formed in early
Palaeolithic times by the silt and mud which the swift-
flowing Nile brought down with it and deposited as it
joined the sea. Secondly, there are a number of oases,
watered, with one exception, by wells or springs which
tap subterranean waters. Thirdly, there is the Nile
valley, which is really a gorge between the cliffs forming
the escarpment, on the one side of the Arabian, on the
other of the Libyan, desert. This valley is quite narrow;
its maximum breadth is about fourteen miles, but in
Middle Egypt the average width is more like nine miles,
and in Upper Egypt it shrinks to a mile or two, in some
places to no more than a narrow strip of cultivation on
one bank only of the river. Egypt is in shape like a tad-
pole with a large head and a very long tail. The length of
this tail, from Cairo to the modern frontier north of
Wâdi Halfa, is about 560 miles as the crow flies, but, if
we allow for the curves of the river valley, about 760
miles; to Aswân, where for long periods, though not
always, ancient Egypt really ended, it is rather less than
550 miles.

All this area is dependent on irrigation for its existence
as a centre of human life. Rain is indeed not infrequent
during the winter in the Delta and at Cairo; it diminishes
in frequency as we go southwards, and at Luxor falls in
any quantity only about once every three years; but in no
district is it sufficiently abundant or regular to maintain
vegetation. It may be taken as broadly true that nowhere in Egypt does a blade of wheat or grass grow which
has not been watered, either by the natural inundation
of the Nile or by artificial means; a piece of waste ground
in an Egyptian town is not grass-grown as with us but is
merely barren sand. This may be seen very strikingly as

one travels by the branch-line from Wâsta in the Nile
valley to Medînet el-Fayyûm. At one point in the
journey there is a sudden rise in the level of a foot or so;
on the lower side of this stretch green and fertile fields, on
the upper there is nothing but a wilderness of sand and
rock.

The oases, which are depressions in the desert plateau,
are watered, as already said, only by wells or springs.
There is one exception, the largest of them and the
nearest to the Nile valley. This is the province of the
Fayyûm, which lies only a few miles from the western
edge of the valley and is irrigated by the Baḥr Yûsuf or
Canal of Joseph, so called because of a legend that it was
constructed by Joseph when he was ruler of Egypt under
Pharaoh. It is in fact a natural branch of the Nile, which
leaves the main stream near Assiût and, after irrigating
the Fayyûm, empties the residue of its waters into the
lake now called Birket el-Ḳarûn, but in ancient times the
Lake of Moeris.[3]

It will be gathered from what I have said or from the
most cursory glance at a physical map that Egypt is a
very isolated country, cut off from the rest of the world
on both sides by formidable deserts. It is thus a difficult
country to invade. I remember being amused, when
Turkey declared war on us in the First World War, at the
attempt of a journalist to allay anxiety by the statement
that Egypt had never been successfully invaded from the
side of Palestine. It would have been nearer the truth to
say, though the statement would still have been inac-
curate, that it had never been successfully invaded from
any other direction. An enemy approaching from the
sea is apt, as the crusading army under St. Louis of
France discovered in 1249–50, and as the 'Peoples of the
Sea' had found long before it, during the reign of

Ramesses III, to find himself entangled in the maze of channels which cut up the Delta. An invader from the west suffers, as Rommel learned to his cost at El-Alamein, from the disadvantage that he is fighting hundreds of miles from his base and with little but desert behind him against an opponent who can draw on all the resources of the Nile valley. There have been, it is true, one or two successful invasions from the west, like the conquest of Egypt by the Fâṭimid Caliphate in A.D. 969 or the expedition of Nicêtas which I shall have to mention in my last chapter; but in general the rule holds true that successful invaders of Egypt have come from the east, across the Sinai peninsula and along the eastern branch of the Nile to where Cairo now stands. From the south there is an access by the Nile valley, but only rarely has there been in the Sudân a power strong enough to threaten Egypt with more than marauding raids; and the narrowness of the gorge above Aswân and the difficulties of navigation caused by the First Cataract make it easy to defend this southern gateway of the country.

The physical peculiarities of Egypt have had an important influence on the growth and character of Egyptian culture. On the growth, since the Nile valley possesses two factors important in stimulating the development of civilization: on the one hand, a soil of immense fertility when properly watered, and reinforced annually by the silt and mud deposited during the inundation, on the other hand, the constant call for effort, and effort of a co-operative kind, to control the water, to conserve it during the period of low Nile, and to survey lands the boundaries of which are every year effaced by the flood. This is not a country in which man can live at ease, merely gathering the fruits which a bountiful nature

offers him without effort of his own; not a country in
which the individual can pitch his dwelling, till his land,
and tend his flock without reference to anyone else; not
a country, finally, in which it requires every ounce of his
energy to maintain the bare essentials of life on an in-
fertile soil and against a rigorous climate. The call for
effort, the promise of a rich return if such effort be made,
and of some surplus on which a stable and secure social
order can be built—it is no accident that Egypt, with
Mesopotamia and the Indus valley, should have provided the basis for the first development of civilization
out of primitive barbarism.

The nature of the country has influenced also the
character of Egyptian culture. Living in their long,
narrow valley and cut off on both sides from the outer
world by great stretches of desert, the Egyptians have
always been a somewhat isolated race, at least before
modern developments in transport. To the south, where
the Nile gorge offered a passage, were races always inferior in culture to themselves; only from the sea and by
way of the Delta had they any links with equal or superior
civilizations. It was natural that their own institutions
should be so largely autonomous, so peculiar, in many
cases, to themselves, and that they should cling with such
tenacity to immemorial usages; natural, too, that they
should develop a certain isolationism of spirit, a national
self-conceit which can be traced in many Egyptian
legends and traditions.

There is a further political consequence which may be
noted. In the long, narrow valley the Nile offers indeed
an excellent highway of traffic, but its stream is swift, and
communication between Upper and Lower Egypt can
never have been very rapid before steam power was
available. The capital in historical times has usually

been either in or close to the Delta or far south in the
Thebaid; in other words, either the northern or the
southern extremity of the country has been remote from
the seat of government. This accounts for a recurring
phenomenon in Egyptian history, the difficulty, when-
ever the central government was weak, of preserving
unity, the tendency of the extremities to break away.

Finally, there is a consequence which has proved of
importance not indeed to history itself but to the historian. The dry soil of Egypt is an unsurpassed preserver
of objects buried in it. Such perishable materials as
paper, parchment, textiles, and wood are inevitably
destroyed, sooner or later, in the moist earth of European
and Asiatic countries; in the sands which everywhere
border the cultivated areas of Egypt they last practically
for ever if the conditions are favourable. Conditions are
not always favourable: the violent winds which blow up
from the desert set the loose sand rolling and flying, and
papyrus texts buried within it are often defaced by fric-
tion; white ants may devour papyrus or linen or wood.
These causes, however, are not always operative, and
we have won from the Egyptian soil a wealth of documents, on papyrus or other materials, far more abundant
than is available for any other country of antiquity.

It is primarily on the evidence of these documents that
the present series of lectures rests; but before I say anything about the documents themselves I must deal with
papyrus as a material and with the history of papyrological discovery. The writing material, the ancient
equivalent of our paper (to which indeed it has given its
name), was made from the stem of the papyrus, an
aquatic plant formerly common in the swamps of Lower
Egypt, though now extinct there. It seems to be supposed by many that it was prepared from the bark of the

plant, but this is an error. The triangular stem of the papyrus contains a fibrous pith with a very sticky sap, and the paper was made by cutting this pith into thin strips, laying a number of these side by side, and then placing upon them a second layer at right angles to the first. The two layers were stuck together by pressure, the sap, with Nile water, being sufficiently glutinous for this purpose; there is, so far as I am aware, no real evidence for the idea that any artificial adhesive was employed. The sheet thus formed, on one side of which the fibres were vertical, on the other horizontal, was hammered with a mallet to soften the tough fibres and was then ready for use as a writing material.[4] But it was not sold separately. A number of sheets (each of which was called a *kollêma*) were stuck together with paste to form a long roll, and it was in this shape that the papyrus left the factory, the purchaser cutting from the roll as much as he required for his purpose. In making up a roll care was taken so to join the single *kollêmata* that all the horizontal fibres were on one side, all the vertical ones on the other. It was the inside or *recto*, on which they were horizontal, which was primarily intended for use, but it was equally easy to write on the outside or *verso*. It was, it is true, very unusual for a text inscribed on the *recto* to run over on to the *verso*, but the use of second-hand papyrus, after the text written on the *recto* had ceased to be needed, was quite common, whether for such purposes as private letters and accounts, drafts and copies of official or legal documents, and memoranda, or for the cheaper manuscripts of literary works, particularly, it may be, for those destined to serve as school-books.

There was one exception to the rule that all the *kollêmata* must have the fibres running the same way. The outside sheet, known as the *prôtokollon* or first *kollêma*, was attached the reverse way, vertical fibres inside, horizontal outside. The reason was that in a large roll there is always a certain pull at the outer end. If at this point the fibres on the outside were vertical there would be a danger of their being pulled apart and of the papyrus disintegrating. By bringing the horizontal fibres of the first sheet to the outside this danger was averted. In the Byzantine and perhaps the Roman age it was customary to write on the inside of the *prôtokollon* an inscription giving the name and title of the official (in Byzantine times the Count of the Sacred Largesses) under whose department the papyrus monopoly[5] fell. In course of time the name *prôtokollon* came to be attached to this inscription and still later was given to the text which followed. Hence our use of the word *protocol*; but the original sense was simply 'first sheet'.

Papyrus was not the only writing material employed in Egypt, still less in the ancient world generally. Prepared skins were used in several countries, including Egypt. From skins, by improvements in the technique, was evolved the finer parchment or vellum, which was to become the chief writing material of the Middle Ages. Vellum plays no part among our finds from Graeco-Roman Egypt before the second century of our era, but from that time onwards it came increasingly into use, and we have numerous specimens from the Byzantine age, mostly literary or theological, but including some documents.

Much commoner was the employment of potsherds. The coarse, porous red pottery used in Egypt and elsewhere took the ink readily; and since broken pots could be picked up on any rubbish-heap there was no material so cheap or handy. Potsherds, or ostraca, were used for all sorts of ephemeral purposes, above all for tax-receipts, but also for private letters, memoranda, accounts, and school exercises. In parts of Egypt where the material was available recourse was also had to slabs of the easily flaked limestone. In museum collections such limestone tablets are lumped with potsherds under the generic name of ostraca.

Yet another material was wooden tablets. These might be used in either of two ways. The characters might be inscribed with pen and ink on the wood, which in that case was often whitened, the better to show up the writing. Alternatively melted wax might be poured on to a wooden tablet with raised edges, forming as it cooled an even expanse on which the writing was incised with a pointed metal implement called a stilus. One end of this was rounded and could be employed to smooth out the wax when the text first written had served its purpose. The fact that tablets could thus be used over and over again made them specially useful in schools. When intended for school use a number of them were often tied together with string, which was passed through holes in the raised edges. The two outermost tablets then had wax only on the inner side, and the whole, known as a codex, looked very much like a modern book. It is indeed from such collections of tablets that both the form and the name of the codex, as distinguished from the roll, were derived. The use of waxed tablets was by no means confined to schools. They were used for memoranda, accounts, drafts of literary compositions, private letters, and for many kinds of legal documents, in particular such instruments as wills, birth certificates, assignments of a legal guardian, and the like. For legal and official purposes employment was made of a diptych, that is to say, of two tablets tied together. The document was written in duplicate, on the inside in wax, on the outside with pen and ink on the wood. The diptych was then tied up and sealed by witnesses, each of whom wrote his name against his seal on the wood. If the authenticity of the outer writing, the *scriptura exterior*, should be challenged in any particular, the seals could be broken and the wording compared with the *scriptura interior*.[6]

Finally, we have, from Egypt as from all the other countries of the Graeco-Roman world, many inscriptions on stone or bronze.

I have said that the soil of Egypt preserves even the most perishable materials buried in it. This statement applies, however, only to certain parts of the country. Papyrus, though a tough and durable material when used with reasonable care, is soon destroyed by damp. It is therefore useless to look for it on any site accessible to the inundation. The whole Delta has thus to be ruled out as a possible source. At Alexandria was the greatest library of the ancient world, and the city was the site of a famous university and the scene of much literary activity. What treasures might we not unearth there if conditions were favourable! But ancient Alexandria is now below sea-level, and no fragment of papyrus has ever been recovered from its soil. We have, it is true, a number of papyri written in the city, but they were all found elsewhere, in places to which, for one reason or another, they had been taken in antiquity.

There are, indeed, two exceptions to the rule that no papyrus is found in the Delta. On the site of Tanis, near its eastern edge, Sir Flinders Petrie found in the winter of 1883–4, in the cellar of a house burned down in antiquity, a mass of papyrus rolls reduced by the heat to the appearance of blocks of charcoal. A similar discovery has also been made on the site of the ancient Thmouis, some thirty-five kilometres to the south-west

of Tanis. The fire which destroyed the houses, in car-
bonizing the papyri, preserved them against destruction
by water, and it has been possible to unroll a number of
them. Thin as gossamers, they can still be read if seen
under favourable conditions of light, and the Greek rolls
from Thmouis have yielded valuable information about
economic conditions in the Mendesian nome during the
second and early part of the third centuries of our era.[7]

Apart from such exceptional cases finds of papyri are
not to be expected in any stratum of soil which has been
regularly irrigated. There is, of course, a level at which
only a slight degree of dampness is perceptible, and in
such strata papyri are sometimes found which have
suffered indeed but have not been destroyed by the
damp. They are darkened to a deep brown, rather like
peat, and the writing, the ink having become irridescent,
can often be read only by holding the document
obliquely to the light.

There are three main sources of papyrus discovery.
The first is the rubbish-heaps which, in ancient as in later
times, grew up near any inhabited place, and often rose
high above the general level. On to them were flung all
the products of human activity which had fallen out of
use, tools, utensils, crockery, and the contents of waste-
paper baskets. Literary rolls were regularly torn to
pieces before being thrown away, but the tearing was not
always very thorough, so that pieces of considerable size
may be found, along with many smaller fragments,
which the patience and ingenuity of scholars have pieced
together. When the modern student reads on the printed
page such works as the *Ichneutae* of Sophocles, the
Hypsipyle of Euripides, the Paeans or the *Partheneia* of
Pindar, or the *Meliambi* of Cercidas, he may not always
realize that, fragmentary as these works are, they were

far more so when first discovered; that many of the longer stretches of continuous text which he sees have been made up from dozens of little fragments. Even tiny scraps, containing no more than two or three letters, can often be placed in their correct position and used to re-construct a large piece. Such work at an unknown text is like doing a jig-saw puzzle to which there is no key and of which half or more than half the pieces are lost.

Documents were not so often torn up before being thrown away. They have, however, usually suffered from the eroding effect of wind-driven sand, the atten-tions of white ants, or the tiresome practice to which native finders sometimes resort of cutting a complete roll into two or even three pieces, which are then divided among the party and sold separately. Thus the majority of papyri found on rubbish-heaps are imperfect; but the number of those which have survived virtually intact is considerable.

A second source is the ruins of ancient houses or other buildings. Here there is a better hope of finding papyri in a more or less perfect state. Expectations should not be pitched too high, since it must be assumed that when a house was abandoned any of the contents to which the occupants attached value would be removed; but not everybody made a complete clearance, and we have to allow for such factors as the collapse of a building or a sudden evacuation. Certain it is that many papyri, some already fragmentary but others in excellent condi-tion, have been recovered from ruins.

The third source is tombs. Here a common miscon-ception must be corrected. When tombs are mentioned in connexion with the discovery of papyri it seems generally to be supposed that the papyri so found had been buried with the dead as part of the grave furniture.

This is in fact true of most hieroglyphic and hieratic papyri. Chief among these is the Book of the Dead, which was a kind of manual for the use of the soul in its journey into the land of Amentit or Hades, containing the necessary formulae and incantations and the correct answers to the questions which the dead man would be asked. It was natural, therefore, that it should be placed with him in the tomb. It was equally natural that if he had been a reader some favourite books should go with him. The Egyptians conceived of life in the next world as very like life on earth, and so the dead were provided with all that was needful, with food and drink and utensils, jewellery and furniture, and *ushabti* figures of servants and workmen to labour for them in their new surroundings. Some Greek papyri seem to have been buried with a similar motive. The roll containing the *Persae* of Timotheus, probably the earliest Greek manuscript that survives and written in the last quarter of the fourth century B.C., was found in a tomb, buried with a dead Greek; so, too, the Hawâra Homer, found by Sir Flinders Petrie, had been laid under a woman's head. It is reported that three famous literary papyri in the British Museum, Aristotle's treatise on the Athenian Constitution, the odes of Bacchylides, and the mimes of Herôdas, had a similar origin; but since they were bought from dealers, who always do their best to conceal the source of their wares, these statements cannot be relied on.

Such cases are exceptional. When I speak of tombs as a source of papyri I am referring to a custom which prevailed at certain periods and in certain parts of Egypt of making mummy cases out of cartonnage, that is to say, layers of papyrus or linen glued together into a sort of papier mâché, moulded to the form of the mummy, and then covered with plaster, which was painted. By breaking up the cases, separating the layers, and removing the paint and plaster it is possible to recover the papyrus, which had generally been used as writing material before being turned over to the case-makers. In this way many texts of great value, both literary and documentary, have been obtained.

The earliest discoveries of Greek papyri were due to the activities of the *sebakhîn* or diggers for *sebakh*. *Sebakh* is the fine, powdery soil which covers ancient sites in Egypt. It is regarded by the Egyptians as a valuable fertilizer and is carried off in great quantities to spread on their fields. Papyri found in the course of the digging should by Egyptian law be reported to the authorities, but needless to say this is practically never done; the papyri discovered are in fact disposed of to dealers and by them sold to foreign buyers or to the Cairo Museum. The first recorded discovery of Greek papyri occurred in the year 1778, when some fifty rolls were offered to a traveller. One of them he bought; the others were burned by the finders, disappointed, we may suppose, by their failure to sell the whole collection. The one survivor, known as the Charta Borgiana because it once belonged to Cardinal Stefano Borgia, is now (or was till the war) in the Museo Nazionale at Naples; it contains a list of workers for the dike-corvée in the year A.D. 192. Further finds were made in the early years of the nineteenth century; about 1820 a valuable collection of rolls dating from the Ptolemaic period was discovered at Sakkârah, on the site of the ancient Serapeum. Other discoveries followed at irregular intervals through the middle years of the century. They included a number of magical texts, one or two rolls of Homer, several of the lost speeches of the Athenian orator Hyperides, and a very interesting *Partheneion* or 'maiden-song' of the Spartan poet Alcman.

These discoveries, though they attracted a good deal of attention in interested circles, were not numerous enough to leave much impression on the world of ancient scholarship in general, but in the later seventies great masses of papyri began to be unearthed in the vast mounds which covered the ruins or formed the rubbish-heaps of Arsinoê, capital of the Arsinoite nome, as the Fayyûm was called in Graeco-Roman times. Large numbers of these papyri were acquired by European buyers, many of them by the Austrian Archduke Rainer. These last became the nucleus of the famous Rainer collection at Vienna; many others went to Berlin, smaller quantities to the Louvre at Paris and the British Museum in London. It was no longer possible for scholars to ignore this new source of information about the ancient world, and from that time a constant stream of papyri began to flow into the museums and libraries of Europe and, later, of America. The first discovery of Greek papyri by a scientific excavator (apart from a very few fragments found among the burnt rolls at Tanis in 1883–4) was made by the late Sir Flinders Petrie in the winter of 1889–90, though it was not for papyri that he was looking. Excavating an ancient cemetery at Gurob in the Fayyûm, he found many mummies enclosed in papyrus cartonnage, which, on being broken up, yielded the remarkable collection known as the Petrie Papyri. It dates from the third century B.C., and besides many documents there were found some valuable literary papyri, among them fragments of a roll containing the *Laches* and *Phaedo* of Plato, written within a century of Plato's death, and another with over a hundred lines of the lost *Antiope* of Euripides. When, in the early nineties, the British Museum made a sensational purchase of papyrus rolls which included Aristotle's lost treatise on the Athenian constitution, another speech of Hyperides, and the mimes of Herôdas, and when, a few years later, these were followed by the poems of Bacchylides, the science of papyrology may be said to have won recognition as a special branch of classical studies, though it did not receive its name till later, and the present editorial technique was evolved only gradually.

In 1895 the Egypt Exploration Society (or Fund as it was then called), feeling that the time had come to include Greek papyri within the range of its activities, decided to send out three Oxford classical scholars, B. P. Grenfell, A. S. Hunt, and D. G. Hogarth, to make a preliminary search. They excavated in the winter of 1895–6 on two sites in the Fayyûm, with results which, though not spectacular, were so far encouraging that in the following winter a concession was obtained to dig at Behneseh, the ancient Oxyrhynchus. The excavators were again Grenfell and Hunt. The finds in that first season were not only good but sensational: large quantities of papyri were unearthed, and the early discoveries included a new poem by Sappho and a leaf of a papyrus codex containing the so-called *Logia* or Sayings of Jesus. In the summer of 1897 the Fund established a special Graeco-Roman Branch. The next winter, instead of returning to Oxyrhynchus, Grenfell and Hunt, fearing that new irrigation schemes might lessen the chances of success in the Fayyûm, returned to that province, where they worked for the next four years, with good results. In the winter of 1899–1900 they excavated for the University of California at Ûmm el-Baragât, the ancient Tebtunis, on the southern edge of the Fayyûm. Anxious to discover Ptolemaic papyri and remembering

Petrie's great find at Gurob, they searched for a Ptolemaic cemetery, and great was the joy in the camp when
one was found. Correspondingly great, therefore, was the
disappointment when, on laying bare a large tomb, it
was seen that it contained only mummies of the sacred
crocodiles; the Fayyûm was the nome of the crocodile
god Sobk. *Bakshîsh* is always given to the diggers for a
good find; and one of the workmen, angry at so poor a
result, gave one of the crocodiles a furious blow with his
spade. It split open and proved to be wrapped in sheets
of inscribed papyrus. As Hunt put it in one of his lectures,
crocodile stock, previously at a discount, rose at once
to a large premium. From this source was derived a
quantity of most important documents dating from the
second and early first centuries B.C., which now fill
volume i of the *Tebtunis Papyri*. In the other two volumes
are published papyri of the Roman period found in the
ruins of the town and those obtained from Ptolemaic
cartonnage of the more usual kind.

After digging at El-Hîbeh in the Nile valley Grenfell
and Hunt returned to Oxyrhynchus in 1903 and continued excavating there until the winter of 1906–7, with
outstanding success. Oxyrhynchus has indeed been the
most productive site in Egypt, especially for literary
papyri. The Paeans and other lost poems of Pindar, new
fragments of Sappho, Alcaeus, and other lyric poets, the
Ichneutae of Sophocles, the *Hypsipyle* of Euripides, substantial portions of several lost plays of Aeschylus, the
Meliambi of Cercidas, considerable fragments of Callimachus, an imperfect but extensive roll containing an
important history of Greece in the early fourth century
B.C., two fragments of the Sayings of Jesus, portions of
several apocryphal gospels, and fragments of what was
until the discovery of the Chester Beatty papyri the

earliest surviving manuscript of St. John's Gospel—
these are but a few of the treasures which the learned
world owes to Oxyrhynchus. After the site had been
abandoned Dr. John Johnson, from 1909 to 1912, continued excavations for the Society in other places.

The British example was not long in stimulating
interest elsewhere. A German expedition dug on the site
of the ancient Heracleopolis in 1899, with good success,
but unfortunately the ship in which the finds were being
conveyed to Germany took fire in Hamburg harbour,
and the whole collection was destroyed. Later other
German expeditions were successful in not only dis-
covering but safely bringing home valuable papyri, and
the French, the Italians, the Americans, a Franco-
Polish expedition, and the Egyptian Service des Antiquités have all taken a hand in the work, while the digging of the *sebakhin*, authorized or illicit, has never
ceased. By now the well-known sites are all virtually
exhausted, and unless others equally productive should
be discovered, which does not seem likely, it is probable
that the supply will soon dry up, except for occasional
single finds. Two such, of sensational quality, both due
not to scientific excavation but to native diggers, have
occurred in fairly recent years. One, made in or about
1931, was of a collection of early Biblical papyrus
codices, now largely but not wholly in the possession of
Mr. Chester Beatty,[8] which must rank in importance
second only to the discovery by Tischendorf of the
Codex Sinaiticus. The other occurred in 1939 or 1940,
and since the papyri in question have not yet been published I cannot say more than that they are likely to
prove of exceptional interest to students of patristic
theology.

It is by no means only Greek and Latin papyri

which have been unearthed in Egypt. Many are in the various forms of the Egyptian language, hieroglyphic, hieratic, Demotic, and Coptic. Numerous Arabic papyri have also been found, besides smaller numbers of documents in other of the various languages which have been spoken by settlers in Egypt. The word papyrology ought, etymologically, to mean the study of any papyri, in whatever language or script, but in fact, unless some distinguishing adjective is used, like 'Coptic papyrology', it is generally applied only to those written in Greek or Latin. But if it is, in one direction, narrower in its application than its etymology suggests, it has, on the other side, a wider denotation, for it embraces all written records, on vellum, ostraca, wooden tablets, and the like, found in Egypt and couched in the Greek or Latin languages. Only the inscriptions on stone or bronze, which fall under the science of epigraphy, are excluded. I should add that, as might be expected, Greek being the official language, Latin papyri are very much rarer than Greek.

The number of Greek papyri published is now large, amounting to many thousands; those discovered, if we reckon the smaller fragments, run into tens of thousands. When Grenfell and Hunt began their work it was possible without any great strain to carry all that was essential to papyrological study in one's head, but this is now quite out of the question for even those best endowed with the faculty of memory, and the literature of the subject is very extensive. Handbooks of various kinds, unnecessary at first, now aid the worker. There is a *Wörterbuch* or glossarial index to the papyrus documents;[9] a *Namenbuch* or index of personal names;[10] a *Sammelbuch*,[11] in which are collected such isolated Greek documents of every class and on every material (including inscriptions) relating to Egypt as have appeared in periodicals or elsewhere; a list of corrections to published texts;[12] and a *Konträrindex*,[13] in which all words found in papyri are printed in reverse alphabetical order (a valuable assistance to a decipherer who sees only the end of a word and wishes to find what supplements are possible). The late Professor U. Wilcken edited till his recent death a special papyrological journal,[14] the Société Royale Égyptienne de Papyrologie issues another,[15] and a third has recently been started in America.[16] Moreover, papyrological articles figure largely in such journals as *Aegyptus* (Milan), *Annales du Service* (Cairo), *Chronique d'Égypte* (Brussels), and *Journal of Egyptian Archaeology* (London). Five international Congresses of Papyrology have been held, and a sixth was under discussion when war broke over Europe in 1939.

Naturally the papyri discovered, chosen as they are by the whim of chance and not by any deliberate selection, are of the most varied character and importance. They range from extensive and well-preserved rolls to quite worthless scraps; they include fragments of literary works showing every degree of merit from the masterpieces of classical writers to the productions of local poetasters in Egyptian villages, and stretching in date from Homer to writers of the sixth century A.D. Christian papyri, whether Biblical or theological, are numerous; pagan religion is represented by several texts; magic is profusely illustrated. Of documents there is every kind, public and private, from copies of royal or imperial edicts to hasty jottings by obscure residents in some unimportant village or the first attempts at penmanship by schoolboys. The period covered by these documents extends from the year

311 B.C., the date of the earliest documentary papyrus yet discovered, till after the end of the first century of the Hegira, say, roughly, to the middle of the eighth century A.D. Among the various classes of documents are royal or imperial ordinances, which often contribute valuable information on administrative or legal policy. The evidence of these single decrees is supplemented by the remarkable rolls edited by Grenfell under the title *Revenue Laws of Ptolemy Philadelphus*,[17] which, among other things, supply precious evidence as to the Ptolemaic oil monopoly, by an equally remarkable papyrus found at Tebtunis,[18] in which a Ptolemaic Finance Minister lays down for the benefit of a subordinate a series of instructions on the financial administration, and, from Roman times, by the so-called *Gnomon* or rules of the financial department known as the *Idios Logos* or 'Special Account'.[19] Official correspondence and the minutes or day-books of administrative officers give us glimpses into the daily routine of government. Tax registers and assessments show the principles of taxation, and innumerable tax-receipts illustrate the system in operation. Land surveys, supplemented by returns of unwatered or waterlogged land and returns of property, enable us to reconstruct in large measure the agrarian policy of successive governments. Census lists and returns reveal the methods of registering and recording, for purposes of administration, the population of Egypt, and their evidence is enlarged by returns of birth and death. Legal documents of all kinds, petitions, reports of lawsuits, marriage contracts, contracts of divorce, contracts of apprenticeship or partnership, sales, leases, loans, mortgages, receipts, orders to bankers, and wills and donations have enormously extended our knowledge of ancient legal systems, as well

as of social life and economic conditions, which are
further illustrated by private letters and accounts, by
the petitions and reports of legal disputes (often containing vivid details), by such documents as inventories
or the specifications of dowry in marriage settlements,
and by wills. Lastly, we have a large quantity of
evidence on education in Graeco-Roman Egypt:
school-books, scholars' exercises, allusions in private
letters.

We have in fact, for Graeco-Roman Egypt, a wealth
of documentary evidence such as exists for no other part
of the ancient world. Such evidence is particularly
valuable owing to the character of our historical sources.
With few exceptions ancient historians were interested
mainly in political events, very little in economics or
social conditions. Even Thucydides, surely the greatest
of all historians, tells us little, and that usually only by
implication, about the social and economic life of his
time. If we desire such information we must turn to
comedy, to the dialogues of Plato, to the speeches of the
Athenian orators; for later periods, and for Rome, to the
correspondence and orations of Cicero, to Horace and
Propertius, to the letters of the younger Pliny, and the
poems of Martial; but only for a few periods and for
limited areas do we find in our literary sources such
evidence as this. From every part of the ancient world
there is a constantly increasing stock of inscriptions; and
the contributions of epigraphy to historical knowledge
have been immense. Yet even inscriptions have not
quite the range and immediacy of contact which we find
in papyri. A document is not normally inscribed on
stone or bronze unless it is regarded as possessing at
least some permanent and public relevance, however
slender that may seem at times to a later generation.

There is something of formality, of 'full dress', about an inscription, whereas a papyrus letter or a series of jottings may reveal to us the spontaneous and unstudied out-pourings of a person quite obscure but, it may be, not the less important to a modern historian because he reveals the point of view of the common man. It is indeed, on the whole, the common man or woman, the undistinguished average of all classes, from the wealthier citizens of Egyptian nome-capitals to village artisans and humble peasants, that we meet in the papyri, and we are thus brought into intimate contact with circles hardly at all represented in the narratives of the political historian or even in such literary works as those I have mentioned. And it is particularly valuable to historical study to be informed about the daily life of the general mass. It is largely the froth on the surface of human existence which political history records; beneath it all, from generation to generation and through all vicissitudes, goes on the ordinary life of man, made up in the main of trivialities not worthy of separate record, such as the papyri reveal to us. In so doing, they help to correct the bias from which that chronicle of exceptional and outstanding events known as history inevitably suffers.

It must, however, be emphasized that the utility of the papyri as a source of historical knowledge has very definite limitations. For one thing, as I began by point-ing out, Egypt has always been a somewhat peculiar country, regarded by men of other lands as alien and exceptional. We cannot always apply to the Mediter-ranean world generally conclusions which we have evidence enough to consider valid for Egypt. Again, the papyri are themselves ill distributed both topographi-cally and chronologically. For the Delta as a whole they are almost entirely wanting; for Alexandria, which is better represented, they are utterly inadequate. There was in Upper Egypt a Greek city, Ptolemais, about which it would be of immense value to have detailed information;[20] but no papyri have been found on the site, and only a few from other sites and an inscription or two afford a flicker of light. Now conditions varied greatly in different parts of the country. What holds good of the Fayyûm may be quite misleading if applied to the Thebaid, and evidence for either may be inapplicable to the Delta. Temporally, too, the evidence is patchy. The fifth century A.D. is a period still not at all well documented; so is the first century B.C. And even in a period from which we have many documents we may find that they apply mainly to one or two only of the areas from which papyri or ostraca have come, while others are ill represented in documents of that date. Thus, in portraying the condition of Egypt in any period in which we have abundant material for one district while for others, reasonably well represented at another time, it is lacking, we may be recording as the general state of the country what is true only of a part and is due there to merely local causes.

There is, moreover, a further caution which must be borne in mind. In studying documents we are often tempted to yield to them a credence which we are more chary of giving to the statements of an historian. It is too readily assumed that though the latter may lie the former give us the truth. There could be no greater fallacy. Documents are often *ex parte* statements; some were written with the deliberate intention to deceive. They, like the assertions of the historian, must be weighed and tested in the light of other evidence, if it is available, or of general probability. And even if it is true, such evidence may easily mislead us. Men do not write petitions or enter into lawsuits in order to show how contented they are; they do so because of some dispute, some grievance, some disturbance of their normal life. When we have read a number of petitions or records of lawsuits from a single place or period we are apt to draw the conclusion that conditions were very unsatisfactory at that time, that officials were all corrupt or incompetent, that the economic position was critical, that litigiousness was a prevalent vice; to forget that for every man involved in such affairs there may have been scores or hundreds who had no serious cause of complaint. The evidence of papyri, in fact, must be compared if possible (unfortunately it is often not possible) with such further evidence as is available: that of archaeology, which may reveal, in housing or furniture or the like, signs of a prosperity not deducible from the papyrus evidence; that of numismatics in its study of monetary hoards; and so forth. When all precautions have been taken and all reserves made the papyrologist must feel very conscious of his own fallibility. It is the exception, not the rule, for a papyrus document to be complete and undamaged. Many of those which may be described as key documents are seriously defective; the texts we use are dependent in greater or less degree on conjectural restoration, nor are difficulties of reading, due either to the rubbing of the papyrus or to the negligence of the script, at all uncommon. The evidence is always imperfect and haphazard; and if the fact that it was selected for us by the chance of preservation and discovery, not by deliberate choice, probably makes it more widely representative, it has the drawback that the documents which have survived may well not be those which a good historian would have chosen as the most significant. The student of papyri is continually dealing with hypotheses, with inferences from evidence often ambiguous and rarely more than partial; and when he puts two and two together he cannot but be conscious that he may be making not four but five or six.

In the course of the three next chapters I shall have to sketch the economic and social development of Egypt over a period of nearly a thousand years. It is impossible, and would be intolerably tedious, to cite the justificatory evidence for every statement made; and I must ask my readers to remember that my survey will of necessity be couched in a dogmatic tone which is not in strictness justified.

It will be apparent from what I have said that papyrology is not an independent science. It is essentially, as the German scholar Wilcken called it, a *Hilfsdisziplin*, a branch of classical studies, and in particular of ancient history, which has indeed its special field and employs its individual technique but which, on the one hand, must rely on external branches of study and, on the other, makes to the sum total of knowledge a contribution which it alone can supply. For the background and setting of the documents with which it deals it is indebted to the historian. It must make use of the inscriptions edited and interpreted by the epigraphist, and, at various periods, of Demotic, Coptic, or Arabic papyri translated by the Egyptologist, the Coptic, or the Arabic scholar. The numismatist can supply valuable assistance in interpreting the evidence of papyri on currency problems, the archaeologist lays bare the material remains of the society in which the papyri were written, the philologist and grammarian help in their linguistic study; above all, the collaboration of the jurist is necessary if the many legal documents are to be rightly interpreted. On the other hand, papyrology supplies to all these other branches of knowledge material of the highest value. He would be a rash and a reprehensible historian of the ancient world who ignored the evidence of papyri. The modern palaeographer, thanks to them, can carry back his study of the Greek script centuries earlier than was possible to his predecessors of the early nineteenth century; the grammarian and phonetician find in the less literate documents invaluable evidence for the development of the Greek language. For the general classical scholar the existing stock of Greek literature has been sensibly enlarged and not a few literary problems have been elucidated by the discoveries in Egypt. The study of ancient law has profited to an extent hardly to be exaggerated by the legal documents preserved on papyrus. And finally, if the papyrologist must often turn for help to Demotic, Coptic, or Arabic studies, workers in these fields are constantly indebted to the materials which he provides.

In fact, we find in papyrology, as in so many other fields of study, the joy and inspiration of common work to a larger end. And this work is and always has been international in character. On the whole papyrology has been singularly free from those bitter feuds and personal or national rivalries which have troubled some branches of study, ancient or modern.

II

THE PTOLEMAIC PERIOD

At the beginning of November 333 B.C. Alexander the Great, who six months earlier had defeated the forces of the Persian satraps on the Granicus, met the army of the Great King himself at Issus, in Cilicia. The disparity in numbers was immense, and the dispositions of Darius were more skilful than those of his generals in the earlier battle, but the genius of Alexander was worth many thousands of troops; and when the day ended the Great King was in mad flight for the interior of Asia, and his army, except the corps of Greek mercenaries, was a demoralized mass of fugitives.

Two courses were now open to Alexander: he could pursue Darius and attempt at once to vindicate the claim he had just made to be the Lord of Asia, or he could leave the Persians to reconstitute their army while he himself consolidated his position in the West. He was but twenty-three years of age, but already he had the brain of a great statesman and a prudent commander, and he decided on the safer though the less spectacular policy. He knew it would take a long time to raise the levy of Asia; on the other hand, he remembered that behind him was the Persian fleet, which he was in no position to challenge, and which might cut off completely his communications with Macedonia. The wise policy was to secure the coasts of the eastern Mediterranean, where the hostile fleet had its bases, and without which it could not long continue to operate. Thus he turned southwards, occupied without difficulty the northern cities on the Syrian coast, captured Tyre after a long and bloody siege, and continued his march towards Egypt.

Before the fall of Tyre he was called on to make a fateful decision. Darius wrote to him offering him the hand of his daughter, a treaty of alliance, and rule over the Persian Empire west of the Euphrates. It was a tempting offer: had it been accepted, still more had Alexander been killed at the Granicus, where only the sword of Cleitus saved him from death at the hands of the satrap Spithridates, the whole history of the world would have been different. But Alexander's aims had expanded since Issus; and when his trusted general Parmenio declared that if he were Alexander he would accept the offer, the reply was merely: 'So would I, if I were Parmenio.'

Egypt had never been a contented or a comfortable member of the Persian Empire. Between the polytheistic, image-worshipping Egyptians and the Persians, with their hatred of idolatry and their monotheistic tendencies, there was a fundamental incompatibility of temperament. Just as France, when at war with England, was wont to give help to Irish malcontents, so did the Greeks encourage and support revolts in Egypt. For a large part of the fourth century B.C. the country had been actually independent, and it was only ten years before Alexander's arrival that the Persians had overthrown the last native Pharaoh. The satrap Mazacês, recognizing the hopelessness of resistance, submitted without fighting, and Alexander entered Memphis, where, like a true Hellene and in striking contrast to the Persians, he paid homage to the native gods, and was apparently accepted without question as King of Egypt. Like a true Hellene also he celebrated the occasion with competitive games and a dramatic and musical festival, at which some of the leading artists of Greece were present. This was in the autumn of 332 B.C. From Memphis he marched down the western arm of the Nile to Canôpus, where, on the strip of sandy ground between Lake Mareôtis and the sea, he founded the Greek city of Alexandria, called after his own name. Thence he went on to the oasis of Sîwah, to consult the oracle of Ammon, the Egyptian god whom the Greeks identified with their own Zeus. Why he did so, what questions he put to the oracle, what answers he received—these are problems which historians have debated ever since and to which we shall never know the correct answer, for Alexander kept his own counsel. He wrote to his mother telling her that he would communicate his secret to her alone after his return; but since he did not go back to Macedonia it died with him.[1]

One thing, however, we do know: the priest of Ammon greeted him as son of the god. To the Egyptian this was the conventional greeting, due to any king of Egypt, such as Alexander now was, but Alexander did not know this. To him Ammon was Zeus, the supreme god of his people, and the incident left a deep and abiding impression on him. With his deeply religious and romantic temperament, he had always felt himself to be under the special protection of heaven; henceforth he conceived himself as the very son of Zeus-Ammon and his campaign as in some sort a divine mission. More and more in the years that followed his ideas matured and expanded. He had landed in Asia as his father's successor, King of Macedon, Captain-General of Hellas, and the chosen instrument of Greek vengeance on the hereditary Persian foe. Now he was himself King of Persia, a half-divine ruler, and his mission was to heal ancient wounds and bridge old gulfs of enmity. After his return to Susa from the victorious campaigns which had led him deep into the Punjab, he staged a great marriage ceremony there, in which he himself married the daughter of Darius and eighty of the leading Macedonians took Persian or Iranian wives. This was not a mere piece of policy; it was a symbolic act, almost a sacrament. It typified his great conception of the wedding of Europe and Asia; for, as Dr. Tarn has shown, we are probably justified in accepting as true the statements of ancient writers that Alexander was the first person to formulate explicitly the idea of the unity of mankind: that all men are brothers, as being all sons of God.[2]

Not one of Alexander's marshals really sympathized with, or indeed understood, his larger conceptions; and when on the 13th June 323 B.C. he died of malarial fever in his thirty-third year his projects were necessarily left incomplete. But he had already accomplished enough to change the course of history, and the mere force of circumstances compelled a mingling of Europe and Asia. The Persian Empire had ceased to exist. From its northern to its southern, its western to its eastern limits, it was now ruled by Macedonians, all of them possessing at least some degree of Hellenic culture and forced to rely for the consolidation and development of their dominions on the help of Greek mercenary troops, Greek scientists, Greek economists and administrators, Greek technicians. Wherever he went Alexander had founded cities on the Greek model, and the process was continued by his successors in Asia. As in the sixteenth century adventurous Spaniards flocked westwards to seek their fortunes in the New World, or, in the seventeenth and eighteenth, men went from Britain to make a career in the East Indies or to settle in the North American colonies, so, during the century which followed Alexander's death, a constant stream of Greek emigrants flowed eastwards and southwards to the lands which Alexander's genius had opened. They took with them their art and literature and traditional way of life, their civic institutions, their gymnasia, their games and festivals. Nor did the spiritual traffic set in one direction only. Far from their Greek homeland and living among Asiatics or Egyptians, the settlers inevitably tended to be assimilated to their environment; and the new rulers, chafe though they might have done at Alexander's policy of treating the Persians as equals, could not but call in their native subjects to collaborate in the work of government and themselves submit to Oriental influences.

Into the wars that followed Alexander's death I need not enter. The issue was at first whether the unity of the Empire could be preserved and who should wield the central authority; later, when the unity had been irrevocably lost, it was a struggle for political and economic hegemony between the succession states. There was one of the marshals who was apparently never tempted to bid for supreme power. Ptolemy, son of Lagus, one of the seven Bodyguards of Alexander, esteeming a good fat bird in the hand worth several in the bush, managed in the settlement after the king's death to secure for himself the satrapy of Egypt, and was content to consolidate his position there, frustrating successfully more than one attempt to overthrow him but only occasionally sallying out from his fastness to assist—not so actively as to run undue risks—whichever party seemed most likely to be victorious. Alexander had expressed a desire to be buried in the oasis of Sîwah, in the temple of his father Ammon. Ptolemy, knowing that Perdiccas, the regent, had other plans, hastily secured the king's body and at once set out with it to his satrapy, burying it, however, not in the oasis but at Memphis, whence his son later transferred it to the famous *Sêma* or tomb at Alexandria. It was a wise precaution. Eumenês, the one Greek among the protagonists in the civil wars, being at a disadvantage as compared with his Macedonian competitors, found it useful to carry with him as a mascot Alexander's tent, which he could represent as still inhabited by his great master's spirit; how much greater was the advantage to Ptolemy, a Macedonian born, of having the actual body of the king!

Ptolemy at first ruled Egypt as a satrap. The earliest dated Greek papyrus yet discovered[3] has the prescript 'In the seventh year of the reign of Alexander son of Alexander, the fourteenth year of the satrapate of Ptolemy, in the month of Dius'; that is to say, the year 311 B.C. On Alexander's death his weak-minded half-brother, Philip Arrhidaeus, was elected joint king along with Alexander's expected son—born a few weeks later—by the Bactrian princess Roxanê. Philip was murdered in 317 by Alexander's mother, Olympias, and Olympias was herself executed later by Cassander, who had made himself master of Macedonia; and in 311, the year of the contract just quoted, Cassander murdered the young Alexander and his mother, Roxanê. There was now no king, but the *de facto* rulers continued to call themselves merely satraps until 306. In that year Antigonus, still upholding the principle of the unity of the Empire, took the royal title, and his rivals, Cassander of Macedon, Seleucus of Syria, and Ptolemy of Egypt, countered by declaring themselves kings of their respective dominions. Thus came into existence the three great monarchies which were to dominate the Hellenistic world until, one by one, they were absorbed into the Roman Empire.

Ptolemy, now King of Egypt, the Pharaoh, and to his Egyptian subjects a god, seems to have been a genial, hearty, but shrewd soldier, a typical Macedonian of the lesser nobility. He was a patron of Greek letters and was not himself without culture. He was the author of a narrative of Alexander's campaigns, now lost but indirectly, since it was used by historians whose works are preserved, one of our most valuable authorities. He pursued in Egypt a different policy from that adopted in Syria by Seleucus, who continued Alexander's practice of founding cities; Ptolemy, equally dependent on Greek assistance, preferred to settle his mercenaries not in cities of the Greek kind but among the Egyptian populace, on the land or in the capitals of the nomes or provinces into which Egypt was divided. These *mêtropoleis*, as they were called, were often towns of fair size, but to Greek conceptions they were really not much more than glorified villages, since, though called by the Greeks *polis*, e.g. Hermoupolis, 'the city of Hermes', or Hêracleopolis, 'the city of Heracles', they had no self-government, no popular assembly or senate, and were subject to the authority of the official charged with the government of the nome. Only one Greek city, called after himself Ptolemais and built on the west bank of the Nile in Upper Egypt, did Ptolemy found; and it, with Alexandria and the old Greek city of Naucratis in the Delta, alone represented in Egypt the traditional Hellenic conception of the self-governing *polis* or city.[4]

It has been assumed that Ptolemy I and his successors, so far from following the policy projected by Alexander, made a difference in principle between Greeks (and *a fortiori* Macedonians) and Egyptians. The former were the *Herrenvolk*, the latter the subject and inferior race, excluded therefore from the army and the higher

administrative posts. It has even been argued that the
substitution, as capital of the country, of Alexandria for
Memphis, where the son of Lagus first settled, and the
removal of Alexander's body to the *Sêma* in the former
city marked the final abandonment of any tendency
which may originally have been shown to make the
Egyptians equal partners in the State.[5] It is probable
that this view needs modification. Some differences
of legal status there certainly were. For example, the
Macedonian troops enjoyed certain privileges; the
corvée or liability for work on the irrigation canals and
embankments was perhaps (though this is not certain[6])
imposed only on the rural Egyptians; and the Greek and
other settlers were organized in *politeumata* or racial
groups with their own laws; but there is really no evidence for such a drastic racial discrimination as the
theory supposes. The early Ptolemies, steeped though
they might be in Hellenic culture, showed, in their
official policy, no interest in abstract theories, economic
or political; they were hard-headed administrators and
business men, anxious to secure to the State which they
had created stability, wealth, and influence in the world.
Their policy was directed by purely practical considerations. At no time since their days of imperial greatness
in the second millennium B.C. have the Egyptians made
first-rate soldiers; hence the Ptolemies, cut off from the
Macedonian homeland which had furnished the nucleus
of Alexander's army, relied for their armies mainly on
mercenary troops, Greeks, Macedonians, Persians, and
Hellenized Asiatics. Ptolemy I inaugurated the policy
of settling as many of these mercenaries as possible in
Egypt, where they received allotments of land, with the
liability to render military service when required.
Again, the growing substitution of a monetary economy,

based on a coined currency, for the older natural economy, based on corn, a process which had already begun under the Persians, naturally called for the help of Greek financiers. Greek scientists and technicians were needed for the land-reclamation schemes of the Ptolemies and for their experiments in scientific agriculture, Greek administrators were employed to build up the elaborate bureaucracy by which the country was administered. The *koiné* or international form of Greek, based on Attic, superseding even the Macedonian dialect, was the tongue of the court, of the army, of the administration; and the kings of the dynasty had their eyes directed outwards from Egypt, to the world of the eastern Mediterranean in which they were ambitious to play a leading part. Egypt, to them, was no more than the basis of their power, their granary, the source of their wealth; and there is no evidence that any Ptolemy before the last Cleopatra ever learned to speak Egyptian.

The Egyptians, then, who had welcomed Alexander as a deliverer, had some reason to feel that under the Ptolemies they were treated, in fact if not in theory, as an inferior and conquered race. Their sense of inferiority was accentuated by social and economic inequality. Some of the superior priests and a few individual Egyptians who received important offices in the administration formed a kind of native aristocracy, but in the main the Egyptians belonged to a lower class in society than the Greek settlers. They were artisans and tenants of royal land, or if they received allotments (*kléroi*) or acquired 'private' land their holdings were usually less than those of the Greeks. In fact, they were in general tenants, employees, the executive and manual as opposed to the administrative and directing class. That they felt their inferiority is undoubted, and many

of them repaid what they regarded as the contempt of the
Greeks with a sullen hostility and, by a natural reaction,
a national self-conceit and scorn for the 'new-fangled'
ways of the settlers.⁷ We have clear evidence, including
some fragments of a patriotic and prophetic literature,
for the existence of an active nationalist party, which
dreamed of a day when the hated foreigner would be
expelled from the country. The bulk of the Egyptians
probably accepted the new order passively enough;
many learned Greek, took Greek names, and made what
profit they could out of the changed conditions. Even
in the third century B.C. we find Egyptians, not indeed in
the very highest administrative posts, but in positions of
some authority. The priestly caste, which was the chief
repository of native traditions and more than once
furnished leaders in popular risings, found their new
rulers at least less antipathetic than the old. The
Ptolemies, though the earlier kings of the line tolerated
no challenge to their authority, confirmed the priests
in their privileges, founded new temples, and enlarged
and embellished the old. It was an Egyptian priest,
Manetho, who, apparently with royal encouragement,
compiled from temple records and traditions a history of
Egypt in Greek, now lost except for fragments but until
the decipherment of the hieroglyphs serving, through
the use of it by surviving writers, as our chief authority
for early Egyptian history. Among the intestine wars
which in the second and first centuries B.C. sapped the
strength of the monarchy were several rebellions of a
patriotic kind, and as early as the third century we hear
of native risings; but at no period was there a general
insurrection of the native Egyptians against their Macedonian rulers, and in the struggles referred to there were
always Egyptians on the government as well as on the

popular side. In 130 B.C. we even find an Egyptian, named Paôs, as governor of the Thebaid, in command of the royal army.

As for the Greeks in Egypt, though the citizens of Alexandria and Ptolemais might cherish their Hellenic traditions and look down on the Egyptians as barbarians, those who settled in the country districts very soon lost any such exclusiveness as they may at first have shown. They intermarried freely with the natives, began to admit Egyptian names into their family nomenclature, and were gradually assimilated in various ways to their environment. The writer of a papyrus letter written in the second century B.C.[8] speaks of her son learning Egyptian as a means of financial betterment. The assimilation was particularly marked in the sphere of religion. The Greeks had always shown themselves tolerant and receptive towards alien deities. Egyptian gods and goddesses were freely identified with those of Greece; and when we read the names of Greek divinities in the papyri we must always ask ourselves whether the reference is not to some Egyptian god or goddess. Indeed, it is probable that the active worship of at least the Olympian gods to a large extent died out among the settlers, to be replaced by a devotion to domestic cults or to Egyptian deities. In 98 and 95 B.C. we find groups of ephebes, Greek youths, educated in accordance with Hellenic traditions, making dedications to the crocodile god of the Fayyûm.

Under the first Ptolemy there appeared a new cult, that of Sarapis, which has been regarded as designed by the king to form a link between his Greek and Egyptian subjects. The question whence it was derived has been much debated. Statements in ancient authors that the cult-statue was procured by Ptolemy I[9] from Sinope or elsewhere in Asia have led to a search for an Asiatic origin, and an attempt has been made to identify Sarapis with the Babylonian Shar-apsi; but after the thorough investigation of the question by Wilcken[10] there seems to be no doubt that the new god was really a Hellenized form of the Egyptian Osorapis. The Apis bull worshipped at Memphis, the best known of all the sacred animals venerated in Egypt, was conceived of as identified in a peculiar degree after death with Osiris, the god of the Other World. He became in fact Osiris-Apis. Osorapis, in Wilcken's view, was not the single Apis bull after death; he was the embodiment of all the dead bulls, from the beginning downwards. There is evidence of his worship in the neighbourhood of Memphis, even by Greeks, before the appearance of Sarapis, and it seems that what Ptolemy did was to raise this local god to metropolitan rank and to represent him, in accordance with Greek conceptions (perhaps with the help of a statue derived from Sinope or elsewhere), as a man of ideal beauty in the prime of life, like the Hellenic Zeus.

An Egyptian deity, invested with all the mysterious glamour which in antiquity, as later, attached to Egyptian religion, yet represented in a human form recalling the supreme god of Hellas—what better meeting-place for Greek and Egyptian could be imagined? Yet if this was really Ptolemy's intention (and the Greeks were surely receptive enough of Egyptian cults to make any such link unnecessary) he failed of complete success. Outside Memphis and Alexandria, the chief centres of the cult, Sarapis seems to have had little appeal for the native Egyptians and not a very great deal more for the majority of the Greek settlers. So local, indeed, was his popularity in Egypt that a reference to him in a private letter is always taken as indicating the likelihood that the writer was an Alexandrian or was writing from that city.[11] Outside Egypt the story was very different, and it seems not at all improbable that Ptolemy's intentions have been misconceived; that, apart from the cult centred in Alexandria, where Sarapis was at once the common deity, the local meeting-ground, as it were, of the motley populace, and a link between this new Hellenic foundation and Egypt, the god was really designed (so to say) for export rather than for internal consumption. Sarapis was to be the patron god of the Ptolemaic empire, and was to enhance its prestige by the addition to the Hellenistic international pantheon of an Egyptian deity. In this Ptolemy was successful. Already in the third century B.C. there were symptoms of that profound spiritual *malaise* which marked the last centuries of paganism. We are, indeed, too ready to conceive of the classical period of Greek history itself as bathed in perpetual sunshine. Even there a 'sense of sin' was by no means unknown; but with the fall of the city-states, the growth of great cities like Alexandria and Antioch, and the establishment of vast military despotisms there was a marked extension of this feeling, and with it grew up a craving for some redemptive religion and for the assurance of a future life which should redress the imperfections of this. It was to satisfy such longings that the old mystery-cults of Greece, those of Demeter at Eleusis, or of Dionysus-Zagreus, had developed, but in this new age it was rather to the Orient that men looked for salvation. The worship of Sarapis, identified with Osiris and accompanied by the latter's wife, Isis, and her son, Hôrus or Harpocrates, spread through the Mediterranean lands and eventually, under Roman rule, reached far-away Britain. It was under the banner of such deities as the Phrygian Great Mother, the Persian Mithras, and the Egyptian Sarapis that, in the third and fourth centuries, paganism was to fight its last battle with Christianity.

Thus the union of Europe and Asia (including, in this regard, Egypt) of which Alexander had dreamed proceeded automatically as a consequence of his military conquests, but hardly along the lines or on that basis of equal partnership which he had planned. The relation was rather that of conquerors and conquered; but if the Orientals, or many of them, adopted Greek speech, Greek dress, and a good deal of Greek culture, the Greeks on their side borrowed much from their Oriental environment, particularly in religion. Especially was this true in Egypt, where most of the settlers were not living in self-contained and self-governing city-states but were dispersed among the native Egyptians in a country remarkably tenacious of its individuality. In this way was formed a mixed culture, Greek and Oriental elements inextricably combined, which provided the seed-ground and indeed the essential presupposition for the rise and diffusion of Christianity.[12] But the amalgam was not a stable one. Hellenism, continually watered down by Oriental influences, could maintain itself only so long as it was actively supported by the government; it was little more than an upper crust imposed upon an immemorial culture fundamentally alien. In Egypt that crust was nowhere thinner than in the Thebaid, the region farthest from Alexandria and the Mediterranean world, in which the influence of the priesthood was strongest, and probably (though here we can speak only conjecturally) containing the smallest number of Greek settlers.

It is now time to describe (necessarily only in very broad outline) the organization of Ptolemaic Egypt. Our evidence on this subject is derived almost wholly

from papyri and similar documents. Papyri dating from
the reign of Ptolemy I are extremely few and, on this
subject, not very informative, whereas for that of his
successor they are both numerous and valuable. Any
description of Egypt in the third century B.C. must therefore rest mainly on evidence not earlier than the reign of
Ptolemy II Philadelphus; but there is no reason to doubt
that he was following a policy initiated by his father.
Our documents come, moreover, chiefly from the Fayyûm, a province in many ways not typical; of the
Thebaid, in the third century, we know little, of the
Delta still less. For the later history of Ptolemaic Egypt
evidence is patchy, fairly good for certain districts and
periods, wholly inadequate for others. But we can
manage to construct a coherent though not a complete
picture of the system existing in the reign of Ptolemy II
and to trace in part its later development.

Even if we disregard wholly those foreign possessions,
Cyrene, Cyprus, Syria, and the Greek cities in Asia
Minor or the islands, which figured so largely in Ptolemaic policy during the third century, Egypt cannot be
described as a unified national state; it was rather a
bureaucratic absolutism composed of very diverse
elements. Alexandria, Naucratis, and Ptolemais were
in form autonomous city-states. In fact, of course, they
were effectively under the royal control, but they had
their own laws, which excluded inter-marriage with the
Egyptians, and possessed all the apparatus of self-
government. The Greek and other settlers in the
country districts were, as I have said, organized in
politeumata, with some (not fully ascertained) organization and their own laws. Lastly there were the native
Egyptians, the upper classes increasingly Hellenized and
tending to mix with the Greek settlers but the peasantry

retaining all their old characteristics and mode of life, using their native language, and making legal contracts in Demotic, the latest form of the Egyptian script. The king's decrees and ordinances took precedence alike over the laws and decrees of the Greek cities, over those of the *politeumata*, and over the old native law under which, for civil purposes, the Egyptians continued to live.[13] Justice was administered for the Greek settlers in the country districts by itinerant courts of *chrêmatistai*; the Egyptians had the courts of the *laokritai* (*laoi* being used in a sense equivalent to our word *natives*), and for civil cases between Greeks and Egyptians there existed, in the third century B.C., a mixed court, *koinodikion*. This disappeared later, and we have a royal ordinance of the year 118 B.C.[14] which provides that in lawsuits between Greeks and Egyptians arising from Greek contracts recourse shall be had to the *chrêmatistai*, but that cases arising from Demotic contracts shall be referred to the *laokritai*. Besides these courts jurisdiction was exercised, particularly in certain cases, like those affecting the royal monopolies, and for certain classes, like the royal tenants, by various officials of the administration.

All these diverse elements were held together by common subjection to the will of the king, the sole source of justice and of all administrative authority. Egypt was the king's estate, the higher administrative officials formed, in a sense, his household, a conception hinted at even by the title of the all-important finance minister, *dioikêtês*, which means literally 'manager'. Egypt had from time immemorial been divided into nomes or provinces, each administered by a nomarch. Under the Ptolemies the functions of the nomarch were in course of time much restricted, till he became eventually no more than a minor financial official, while the *stratêgos*, at first always a Greek, originally appointed in each nome to command the military forces stationed there, was soon given civil and financial functions and eventually became the actual governor of the nome. Below him and acting as deputy in his absence was the royal secretary; and there were secretaries for the subdivisions of the nome and for single villages.

In this great estate the most valuable element was the land, a soil of unsurpassed fertility when properly irrigated and annually renewed by the rich mud which the inundation leaves behind. In theory the king was the sole landowner, and much of the best land was actually retained under his control. This was the so-called 'royal land', leased to peasants known as 'royal tenants'. The leases were free contracts, though in times when voluntary offers were hard to obtain compulsion was sometimes resorted to, and the royal tenants were free men, not serfs, but their liberty was of a restricted kind; they were not allowed to leave their holdings while agricultural operations were going on, and we hear of peasants moved to other areas where new land was being developed. The State, moreover, could at any moment cancel a lease and transfer the land to another tenant who made a higher bid. On the other hand, the royal tenants enjoyed certain privileges and a measure of government protection.

Though the king, however, was theoretically the sole owner, he was not the only possessor of land, and a degree of private property can be discerned even in the earlier Ptolemaic period, still more in later times. Land not under royal control was described as 'in relinquishment' (*en aphesei*). Thus, the estates which the temples had always possessed, though the actual management of them was taken over by the Ptolemies, were administered

for the benefit of the temples, and formed a special category of 'sacred land'. Other land, as already said, was
granted in allotments (*klêroi*) to the military settlers, who
were known as *klêrouchoi*. By this institution the Ptolemies
attained two desirable ends. On the one hand, making
the grant of an allotment dependent on liability to
military service, they secured a supply of trained soldiers,
with a stake in the country and therefore less likely to
transfer their services to another master than the mercenaries engaged in the open market. On the other
hand, they secured a considerable extension of the cultivated area. They did, it is true, assign fully cultivated
land for this purpose, and this may indeed at first have
been the regular practice,[15] but more often, and with
increasing frequency as time went on, the allotments
were of inferior or derelict land, and the grants were
conditional on its being reclaimed and put under cultivation, though the reclamation might not always be,
and perhaps was not often, carried out by the cleruchs
themselves. The allotments were for life only, but since
it was to the king's interest to retain a supply of military
settlers it became usual for a cleruch's eldest son to
receive the *klêros* on his father's death, and we even find
allotments made in perpetuity.[16] Thus the holdings
tended more and more to become hereditary and so to
acquire an appearance of ownership; but theoretically
it is not likely that, in the Ptolemaic period, they ever
became more than possession, though subterfuges were
found by which alienation became possible. Grants of
large estates, known as *dôreai*, to high officials and royal
favourites might also involve the obligation to reclaim
derelict land. Such grants too were made for life only,
and on the holder's death the land reverted to the
Crown. The cleruchs were often billeted on the local

residents, their billets being known as *stathmoi*. Finally, we hear of so-called 'privately owned land' (*gê idioktêtos*). This, normally at all events, consisted of vegetable gardens, orchards, palm-groves, and vineyards, all of them involving some degree of reclamation and capable of being grown on soil not suited to the cultivation of corn, and the land was probably conveyed in hereditary or long-term leases. Here, too, though legal transfers occurred, it is unlikely that actual ownership ever developed in Ptolemaic times. In fact, as Dr. Tarn puts it,[17] private land in the Ptolemaic period was 'not property but user'.

In this way the early Ptolemies made extensive additions to the cultivated area of Egypt. Our evidence on this subject relates mainly to the Fayyûm or Arsinoite nome during the reigns of the second and third Ptolemies, and is derived very largely from the Petrie Papyri, which include the papers of Cleôn, master of the works for the great reclamation schemes of Ptolemy Philadelphus, and from the archives of Zênôn son of Agreophôn, who about the same period was the agent of the finance minister Apollônius on his gift-estate (*dôrea*) of 10,000 arourae at Philadelphia.[18] All the resources of Greek engineering science were brought to bear on the work of irrigation and land reclamation. Scientific agriculture made it possible in some cases to obtain as many as three crops in a year (incidentally, the remark, in a memorial from some peasants, that 'there are lots of blunders in connexion with the 10,000 arourae, because there is no agricultural expert. Call some of us and hear what we have to say',[19] may suggest that the quarrel between the practical and the scientific farmer is no new thing). Greater variety was given to Egyptian agriculture by the introduction of new crops or the extension of old ones. Viticulture had been practised in parts of Egypt even under the Pharaohs, but the national drink of Egypt was barley beer. The Greeks were wine-drinkers, and the Ptolemies actively encouraged the planting of vineyards on the less fertile land. The vine-growers were protected by heavy duties on imported wine. Olive-planting was also forwarded. The olive, like the vine, had been cultivated in Pharaonic Egypt, but chiefly for eating. After the settlement of the Greeks, for whom the olive was of primary importance, there was a great extension of olive-yards, and olive-oil (which, however, if we can believe Strabo, was of inferior quality) was manufactured in considerable quantities and was protected by a high tariff on imported oil. New strains of wheat were established; garlic and better varieties of cabbage were introduced. Fruit-trees of many kinds were planted; there was a large-scale cultivation of roses, and probably of other flowers, for the garlands which the Greeks wore at banquets; new breeds of animals, particularly of sheep producing better wool than the native variety, were imported to improve the existing strains; the camel was perhaps now first effectively naturalized in Egypt;[20] bee-keeping was extended, and pig-breeding (for the benefit of the Greek settlers and the court, since for the Egyptians the pig was an unclean animal) assumed a new importance. Egypt has always been poor in timber, and the Ptolemies did something to remedy this deficiency also. Thus Apollônius writes to his agent Zênôn: 'Plant fir-trees, over 300 of them if possible, and at any rate not less, all over the park and round the vineyard and the olive-groves; for the tree has a handsome appearance and will be to the advantage of the king.'[21]

The royal activity was not confined to agriculture. A full monetary economy was established in a country which hitherto had depended mainly on a system of barter. A regular coinage was established by Ptolemy I, in gold, silver, and copper. In later times this coinage underwent successive modifications, into which there is no time and no need to enter, and the ratios between gold and silver and silver and copper varied at different periods. Banks were established, and a well-developed banking system can be traced in our records.[22] Yet the old natural economy did not wholly cease: the rents for the royal land and some salaries were paid in kind, nor was barter by any means eliminated from commercial life. The state granaries (*thêsauroi*) which collected the grain served also, like the banks into which money taxes were paid, as repositories for private accounts. In the Roman period, though possibly not under the Ptolemies, payments, both in money and in grain, were regularly made by the mere transfer from one account to another in the books of the bank or *thêsauros*, even where different banks were concerned; and documents which can not improperly be compared with the modern cheque are found among surviving papyri of that age.

There was an extensive system of state monopolies, which, in accordance with the severely practical and un-theoretic policy of the Ptolemies, were variously organized to suit varying needs. Banking was among them, and side by side with the royal banks, which undertook private as well as state business, there seem to have been private banks,[23] leased by the government to individuals. The monopoly about which we know most is that of oil, concerning which we have much information in the papyri published by Grenfell under the title *Revenue Laws of Ptolemy Philadelphus*. From of old, oil-producing plants, sesame, croton, linseed, safflower, and colocynth, had been grown in Egypt. Under the Ptole-

mies the cultivation of these plants was strictly controlled, the government fixing the amount of land to be
set aside for the purpose in each nome and keeping an
eye on the sowing and gathering of the crops. The seed
was supplied by the government to the farmers; the
produce was carefully calculated, a quarter being paid
as tax, the rest delivered by the cultivators at a fixed price
to the contractors. The oil was extracted in factories
under public control, the workers in which, though free
men, not slaves, were not permitted to leave their homes
during the season. Private mills, which had existed
before the new régime was established, were now pro-
hibited, except in the case of the temples, which were
allowed, for two months in the year only, to make their
own oil; during the rest of the year their mills, like the
royal mills when not actually working, were sealed.
The right of sale was farmed out to wholesalers and re-
tailers, who must, however, sell it to the public at a price
fixed by the government. This price was very high, and
the king made an enormous profit, which Dr. Tarn
calculates at a figure as high as 'from 70 per cent. on
sesame oil to 300 per cent. or more on colocynth'.[24]
There was an import duty of 50 per cent. on olive oil,
which was apparently not included in the monopoly.

Another monopoly was that of textiles, alike of linen,
wool, and hemp. The temples were allowed to continue
the manufacture of the fine linen (*byssos*) for which they
were famous, chiefly for their own use (priests were forbidden to wear woollen clothing), but they had also to
deliver a fixed quantity to the king for purposes of
export. Among other monopolies were those of salt,
natron, and beer, the traditional beverage of the
Egyptians; but the home brewing of beer was perhaps
allowed.

From these monopolies, and from the rents of the domain land, the Ptolemies derived a large revenue in money and in kind, which was augmented by numerous taxes. There were taxes on cleruchic and other 'relinquished' lands, a succession duty on estates, licences for the practice of various trades, taxes on sales, on many articles of use, on house property, on the revenues from the exercise of ecclesiastical offices, and a poll-tax of some kind, about the nature of which, however, scholars are not agreed. Finally, there was an elaborate system of tolls and customs duties, some of which, like the duty on imported oil, were definitely protective, while others were for revenue purposes only. The method of collecting taxes, except those payable in kind, for which the government's own officials were responsible, was that of tax-farming, the right to collect the various taxes being put up for auction each year and assigned to the highest bidder. The tax-farmers were strictly controlled at every stage, in the interests of both the Crown and the tax-payers, and it cannot have been easy to make any great profit on the transaction, though at first it seems to have been easy enough to find bidders; later this became increasingly difficult.

Foreign trade was actively stimulated by the Ptolemies. Rich though she is agriculturally, Egypt is poor in many products and has to seek them abroad. Among her imports in the Ptolemaic period were timber, metals, wine and olive-oil, pickled fish, fruit of various kinds, cheese, slaves, and horses. To pay for these her most valuable export was corn, for she was the principal granary of the eastern Mediterranean; but she also exported papyrus, of which she was the sole purveyor to the whole ancient world, the fine *byssos* linen, glass, especially the polychrome glass for which Alexandria was to become famous, alabaster, and other varieties of stone. She had an active transit trade: from Somaliland and East Africa, from Arabia and the Indies came gold, precious stones, pearls, ivory, spices, pigments, certain rare woods, cotton, and silk. Carried overland from the ports of the Red Sea by desert routes to Coptos in the Nile valley, for which purpose, as well as for internal transport, the Ptolemies, as already said, were probably the first to make camels available in Egypt, these wares, when not straightway re-exported, were made up into more finished products by the skill of the Egyptian craftsmen, for internal use or for later export.

The principal port and greatest commercial and manufacturing city in Egypt was Alexandria, the most successful of all Alexander's foundations. Doubtless Alexander acted on advice obtained locally, but it was the eye of genius which saw in the wretched fishing-village of Rhacôtis the site of a great city. Designed by the Rhodian architect Dinocratês on the latest town-planning principles, Alexandria occupied a narrow strip of sandy ground between Lake Mareôtis and the sea. Out at sea was the island of Pharos, which, when connected by a mole with the mainland, formed a safe and spacious harbour on the eastern side and a larger but more exposed one on the western. In the western part of the city was incorporated the old Rhacôtis, which now formed the native Egyptian quarter; a few miles to the east was Canôpus, which became a popular pleasure resort, with a very doubtful moral reputation. The city was rectangular in plan. From east to west ran the broad straight Canopic street, bordered with shady colonnades and intersected by other spacious streets. There were five quarters, called after the first five letters of the Greek alphabet, alpha, bêta, gamma, delta, epsilon.

From the first the population was mixed. The nucleus was the full citizen body, Greek or mainly Greek in blood, and organized like a typical Greek city-state, in tribes and demes, with a senate, popular assembly, and the usual magistrates. Under the Romans, till the reign of Septimius Severus, there was no senate. It is a matter of dispute whether Augustus found one, which he abolished. Personally I believe that Alexandria had no senate at the time of the Roman conquest, but it is hardly thinkable that Alexander should have founded a city without one,[25] and we must conclude that a later king during one of the many conflicts between crown and city abolished it. The Macedonians as a whole do not seem to have formed part of the citizen body, though the original colonists no doubt included Macedonians; some at least of them formed an *élite*, providing the regiments of the guard, the court, and certain of the higher officials. There were many Greeks from other parts of the ancient world who settled in Alexandria but did not acquire its citizenship; there was a large Egyptian population; and among other foreign settlers the Jews were an important element. They were assigned as their residence the Delta quarter, near the royal palace, but spread later till they came to occupy most of a second quarter; indeed Philo tells us that in his time their synagogues were to be found in every part of the city. They were not citizens, but they enjoyed special privileges, with their own lawcourts, their own record office, their council of elders, and a magistrate known as a genarch or an ethnarch. On the quays and in the streets of the city was to be seen a motley crowd, drawn from many races and speaking many languages and dialects. In his *Adoniazusae* Theocritus has given us a vivid picture of this crowd. Says the stranger as the two women talk: 'My good woman, do stop

that everlasting prattle, like a couple of doves. They wear
me out with their broad Doric.' To which the lively
Praxinoa replies: 'Good gracious, where *does* the fellow
come from? What is it to you if we do prattle? You buy
your slaves before you order them about! It's Syra-
cusans you're giving your orders to. . . . I suppose
Dorians are allowed to speak Doric?' Even Indians
appeared in Alexandria, especially after the discovery
(probably early in the Roman period)[26] of the monsoon,
which made it possible to sail direct from Africa to India
instead of hugging the coast; but already in the reign of
Ptolemy II Asoka, the Buddhist emperor of India, sent
to the king his missionaries with their tidings of Deliverance. One wonders what response the teaching of the
gentle Gautama found in the heart of the worldly and
pleasure-loving Ptolemy.

Alexandria was soon the wonder of the world, especially when it became, at an unascertained date, the
capital in place of Memphis. On Pharos rose the famous
lighthouse which has given its name to similar structures
in several modern languages. In the so-called *Sêma* lay
the body of Alexander the Great; in the Rhacôtis
quarter—significantly, as confirming the idea that
Sarapis was an Egyptian deity—was the not less famous
Serapeum.[27] The splendid Gymnasium, the Stadium
and the Hippodrome, the theatre, and the royal palace
were other notable buildings. The palace stood on a
small peninsula to the east of the harbour, and close to it
were the Museum and the Library. The Museum was
primarily a temple of the Muses; in actual fact it was a
combination of something like a modern academy and a
university. Here were established a number of scholars,
scientists, and literary men who enjoyed free board and
lodging and were exempt from taxation. For their use

the Ptolemies collected a vast library of books, which eventually contained something like half a million rolls. In order to enrich the collection Ptolemy III issued an order that all travellers disembarking at Alexandria must deposit any books contained in their baggage, which, if required, were taken by the Library, the owner receiving in exchange an official certified copy. It is also recorded that he borrowed from Athens the state copies of the works of Aeschylus, Sophocles, and Euripides in order to have transcripts made from them, paying as a guarantee of return the large sum of fifteen talents,[28] but that he preferred forfeiting this sum to the return of the originals, in place of which he sent to Athens only copies. In the Library were founded the sciences of bibliography and textual criticism; catalogues of classical Greek literature were compiled, the texts of Homer and other authors were cleansed of many corruptions and established in a form transmitted with comparatively little change to modern times, the system of accentuation so often cursed by the modern schoolboy and undergraduate, and the more welcome punctuation-marks were invented. Nor were science and mathematics neglected. It was at Alexandria that Aristarchus,[29] anticipating Copernicus, guessed the earth's movement round the sun, here that Eratosthenês measured (correctly to within fifty miles) the circumference of the globe, that Euclid wrote his *Elements*, and that Hêrôn invented, or described from another's invention, the steam-engine and the penny-in-the-slot machine. The medical school of Alexandria was famous, especially in anatomy and surgery; and it was in Alexandria that the Greek translation of the Old Testament known as the Septuagint was made for the Jews of the Diaspora, and that Philo promulgated his doctrine of the Divine Logos.

There can be no doubt that Ptolemaic rule at first brought Egypt a great increase in wealth and prosperity. A strong and able administration, which kept order, an improved irrigation system, leading to a vast increase in the cultivable area, a wider variety of crops, making full use of the less fertile land, encouragement to industry, a great extension of foreign trade—these were substantial benefits. But the maintenance of this prosperity after the first burst of energy was spent depended on two uncertain factors: on the one hand, a continued capacity in the government, on the other the willing and active cooperation of the governed. So far as the Egyptians were concerned this last factor was probably never forthcoming. Individual Egyptians may conceivably have welcomed the new régime with enthusiasm, and many undoubtedly contrived to make their profit out of it, but the reaction of the peasantry as a whole, especially in Upper Egypt, seems to have been one, at best of passive acquiescence, at worst of sullen resentment. It may be doubted whether the average Egyptian peasant was very conscious of any marked betterment in his lot. For centuries he had toiled and paid his dues to king, to priesthood, to his landlord. He continued to do so under the Macedonian dynasty, and in so far as the new government secured internal peace and kept off famine he derived some benefit from it, but he never felt himself a partner in the State. His new masters were alien and far away; their policy, directed outwards to the Mediterranean world, pursued ends beyond his comprehension, and the glory of Alexandria, that foreign city which was hardly even a part of Egypt (it was officially described, at least in later times, as 'adjoining Egypt') meant nothing to him. The abler Ptolemies naturally took measures for the prosperity of their estate, but their care for it was at best enlightened self-interest; their aim was, as Mlle Préaux has put it, 'to accumulate the maximum amount of wealth, to incur the minimum of expenditure, to make the fewest possible changes in the existing order, to take the fewest possible risks'. It was doubtless a prudent if unheroic policy in the manager of an estate, but a nation is never just an estate; it is an assemblage of human beings, with individual rights and needs, and something more than economic acumen, some moral purpose, is needed if this mass is to be bound together in a vital unity. To quote Mlle Préaux again, 'an economic conception can never constitute a moral end'.[30]

Thus, as the character of the ruling line deteriorated, the strength and prosperity of the kingdom declined. The first three Ptolemies were all able rulers. Ptolemy II, magnificent, pleasure-loving, of softer fibre than his father, stood to him in somewhat the same relation as Solomon to David, but the papyri show that he possessed both energy and marked administrative capacity. Some of this he may have owed to his sister Arsinoê, who, after she had procured the banishment of his wife, also called Arsinoê, became his legal wife. To Greek sentiment marriage of full brother and sister was almost as shocking as to ours, and it required all the art of the court poets and propagandists to make it palatable.[31] Yet the second Arsinoê, a true prototype of the women of her house, strong-willed, capable, and untroubled by scruples, proved a very useful partner on the throne, and she was quite willing to overlook her husband's numerous infidelities. She received the epithet Philadelphos, 'Brother-loving', and when, after her death and deification, Ptolemy was associated with her in these divine honours their cult-title was *theoi adelphoi*, the 'Fraternal Gods'. Ptolemy I had been deified as Sôtêr, 'the

Saviour'; and Ptolemy II's son and successor received the epithet Euergetês, 'the Benefactor'. Thenceforward all the kings of the dynasty, all of them called Ptolemy, bore a cult-title, under which, even during their lifetime, they were worshipped.

With the fourth Ptolemy, Philopatôr, 'the Father-loving God', a catastrophic decline set in. Philopatôr, described in a priestly inscription as 'the youthful Horus, the strong one, whom his father caused to be manifested as King, Lord of the asp-crowns, whose strength is great, whose heart is pious towards the gods, who is a protector of men, superior to his foes, who maketh Egypt happy, who giveth radiance to the temples, who firmly estab-lisheth the laws which have been proclaimed by Thoth the Great-Great, Lord of the Thirty Years' Feasts, even as Ptah the Great, a King like the Sun, King of the Upper and Lower Countries, offspring of the Benefactor Gods, one whom Ptah hath approved, to whom the Sun hath given victory, the living image of Amen, King Ptolemy, living-for-ever, beloved of Isis',[32] was in reality a weak and contemptible debauchee, completely in the hands of his unscrupulous minister Sôsibius, his vile mistress Agathoclea, her viler brother Agathoclês, and their ghastly mother Oenanthe, as sordid a gang of scoundrels as ever governed an empire until the rise of the Nazis.[33] Absorption in degrading pleasures led to neglect of both army and navy, and when Antiochus the Great, the ambitious and able King of Syria, attacked the Syrian possessions of Egypt there was really no force in the country capable of withstanding him. By skilful diplomacy (whatever his morals Sôsibius was un-doubtedly clever) Antiochus was held off while prepara-tions were made. Mercenaries were hired, the military settlers called up and put through a course of intensive training, the army was completely reorganized, and the Egyptians, hitherto used merely as militia and second-line troops, were armed and drilled on the Greek and Macedonian model as a phalanx. The result was that when Sôsibius, throwing off the mask, refused the demands of Antiochus and the latter resumed his advance the Egyptian forces won a decisive victory in the Battle of Raphia, on the 22nd June, 217 B.C.

Raphia proved, however, a doubtful benefit. The Egyptians, for the first time treated as the military equals of the Greeks, had acquired a new conceit of themselves, and thenceforth there were frequent revolts, largely, though by no means entirely, in the Thebaid, always the breeding-ground of Egyptian nationalism. It would have been possible to cope with this nationalist movement more effectively had it been the only difficulty, but for much of the second and first centuries B.C. the Ptolemaic dynasty was torn by internal quarrels, and Egypt was under constant menace from outside. There had arisen a power which overshadowed the whole Mediterranean world and produced in all the Hellenistic monarchies a sense of insecurity. At first this new power operated to the benefit of Egypt. As early as 273 B.C. Ptolemy II had concluded a commercial treaty with the Roman republic; and when, after the victorious conclusion of the Second Punic War, Rome became involved in the affairs of the eastern Mediterranean she found Egypt a useful counterweight to the power of Syria. The relationship between the two states was by no means disinterested on either side, but it did on occasion prove very useful to Egypt.

Danger from without and constant unrest within, whether in the form of dynastic dissensions or in that of native revolts, were accompanied by, and themselves greatly contributed to, an economic decline which began as early as the reign of Ptolemy IV Philopatôr. Philadelphus had instituted a regular copper currency, side by side with that in gold and silver, thus establishing a trimetallic system, the copper coinage circulating specially among the Egyptians, that in the precious metals mainly among the Greeks. Under Philopatôr a new copper standard was introduced, with a ratio between silver and copper of 1 : 60. Under his successor and later we find periods of inflation, leading to a shrinkage of the revenue and consequent pressure by the officials on the populace, a pressure answered by discontent, passive resistance, and actual revolt. The kings might attempt to check abuses, but their power over the local officials was limited,[34] and it is clear that in the second half of the second century B.C. economic distress, misgovernment, and unrest were widespread; and along with this went a decline in foreign commerce. The growing impotence of the central government led to local separatist movements, concessions to the power of the priesthood, and frequent surrender to pressure from powerful individuals or the mass resistance of the peasantry, in fact to a state of things recalling such periods of disintegration as the period of the nineteenth Pharaonic dynasty and anticipating that of the early Byzantine period.[35]

In 202 Philip of Macedon and Antiochus of Syria, taking advantage of the accession of a boy king, Ptolemy V Epiphanês, the 'God Manifest', formed an alliance to despoil Egypt of her foreign possessions. Her Syrian territories were overrun by Antiochus, her possessions in the Aegean conquered by Philip without any protest from Rome, but it is not impossible that Roman influence played a part in preventing Antiochus from attempting to attack Egypt itself. In 170 B.C., when the ministers of the young king, Ptolemy VI Philomêtôr, the 'Mother-loving God', suffered a crushing defeat in an attempt to recover the lost Syrian possessions, Antiochus Epiphanês, using the occasion of Rome's entanglement in a conflict with Macedon, did invade Egypt and, as we now know from papyrus evidence,[36] actually had himself crowned king. His enjoyment of the title was brief, and eventually, in 168, after the final defeat of Macedon, Rome sent her ambassador, Gaius Popillius Laenas, to demand his withdrawal. When Antiochus tried to procrastinate, the ambassador with his staff drew round him a circle in the sand and declared that an answer must be given before he left it. Rome's diplomatic methods were at times unmannerly, not to say brutal, but her power was too formidable to be defied, and Antiochus, swallowing his anger, submitted. From that time onwards, especially after Syria, like Macedon, had passed into the Roman dominions, Egypt retained her independence only because it did not yet suit Rome's book to swallow her.

By the last century of Ptolemaic rule the native Egyptians, helped by the growing weakness of the government and the need felt by rival claimants to the throne for popular support, had acquired a position much nearer to equality with the Greeks than they had enjoyed under the early Ptolemies. We hear of Egyptians in quite high positions, civil and military; Egyptian veterans received allotments of land like those of the Greeks, though regularly less in area; temple after temple secured from the government the privilege of asylum. This rise in status did not improve relations between them and the Greeks; indeed, with an increased sense of their own importance and a diminished respect for the settlers, their hostility may well have grown. It is probably symptomatic that Ptolemy, the Macedonian recluse whose papers form a large part of the Serapeum papyri, in the middle years of the second century, several times complains of attacks made on him 'because I am a Greek'; and we know that prophecies were current promising the expulsion of the foreigner and the destruction of Alexandria. The Greeks, on their side, though by this time mixed in blood and in various ways Egyptianized, clung, perhaps all the more for that reason, to their Hellenic traditions, the sports of the palaestra, their gymnasia, the institution of the ephebate; and if their surviving letters betray practically no interest in literature or art, we know, from the texts discovered in Middle Egypt, that the Greek classics, Homer pre-eminently but also the dramatists, the orators, the philosophers, the lyric poets, continued to be studied. Yet we must not exaggerate racial animosities; we have plenty of evidence for friendly and even intimate relations between Greek and Egyptian.

For long periods in the second and first centuries Egypt was in the throes of civil war, and at times the Thebaid seems to have been practically independent of the government at Alexandria. In 85 B.C. an obstinate rising ended with the virtual destruction of Thebes, the half-legendary capital of Egypt in the days of her greatness; and 'hundred-gated Thebes', as Homer called her, became, what she has ever since remained, little more than a group of villages scattered among the ruins of her former magnificence.

In the last years of her independence Egypt once more became a factor in Mediterranean politics, and the dynasty produced in its latest representative a figure whose fame is world-wide. The often-quoted remark of

the Victorian lady after witnessing a performance of
Antony and Cleopatra, 'How unlike the home life of our
own dear Queen!' not inaptly represents the view taken
of Cleopatra by the general public, but if we regard her
merely as the super-harlot whom Shakespeare, in
accordance with tradition, depicts, still more as the
kittenish adolescent of Shaw's *Caesar and Cleopatra*, we
shall not only be doing her a grave injustice, we shall be
getting our historical perspective seriously out of focus.
The greatest of the successors of Alexander the Great—
so she has been characterized by our foremost living
authority on the Hellenistic period. It is a high claim,
but it was not made without reason. Cleopatra has been
too long viewed through the distorting medium of
official Roman propaganda. Whatever her moral fail-
ings, she was a woman of outstanding genius and a
worthy opponent of Rome; for, as Dr. Tarn has well
said,[37] 'Rome, who had never condescended to fear any
nation or people, did in her time fear two human beings;
one was Hannibal, and the other was a woman'.
Dr. Tarn seems very probably to be right[38] in referring
to Cleopatra a Sibylline oracle which foretells the overthrow of Rome by an unnamed *despoina*, a queen, who
is to inaugurate a golden age:

'Tranquil peace shall foot it over all the Asian land, and
Europe then shall be happy, a fruitful clime many a long
year, strongly established, that knows nor storm nor hail,
bearing all things, both birds and beasts that go upon the
earth. . . . For from the starry heaven will all fair order and
righteousness come upon men, and therewith concord with
temperance that is for mortals beyond all riches, love
and faith and friendship among strangers, and afar will
flee from men in those days poverty and constraint, law-
lessness, reproach, envy, anger, folly and murder and

baneful strife and bitter wranglings and nocturnal theft and every evil.'

The Messiah who is to establish this age of gold is, it seems, none other than the wayward strumpet of popular tradition! What were Cleopatra's own conceptions, who shall say? She may or may not have loved Antony, as he most certainly loved her; her main preoccupation was doubtless to preserve the independence and if possible extend the territory of Egypt and secure the throne for her children, and to use Antony's infatuation to that end; but to many Orientals she was the symbol of resistance to Rome and the promise of deliverance from her yoke. The apparent tortuousness of Roman policy was probably due at times more to irresolution and the varying currents of party politics than to deliberate duplicity, but the East took a less favourable view, and the government of the provinces by the now decadent republic had long been marked by oppression and spoliation. Thus all the resentment, the hatreds and hopes of many decades found a rallying-point in Cleopatra. But she failed as Hannibal had failed. After Actium Antony, abandoned by his friends and sunk in a stupor of despair, was of no more use to her, and though she abated no jot of her own spirit, her material resources were now quite inadequate. There was nothing for it but to die or to be led in triumph through the streets of Rome, and faced by such a choice she could not hesitate. 'Is this well done?' asked the Roman soldier of the dying Charmion when he found the queen dead between her women; and Charmion's answer, as accurately rendered by Shakespeare, was

> It is well done and fitting for a princess
> Descended of so many royal kings.

Cleopatra's choice of the snake which was to give her release from captivity was significant.[39] It was an asp, the Egyptian cobra, the sacred snake of Lower Egypt. As Pharaoh, Lord of the Two Lands, Cleopatra had worn the double crown, the vulture crown of Upper, the cobra crown of Lower, Egypt. The cobra was the minister of the sun-god, whose bite conferred not only immortality but divinity. Cleopatra had taken the royal road to death and joined the company of the gods, and nothing remained for Octavian but to incorporate Egypt in the dominions of the Roman people.

III

THE ROMAN PERIOD

'I ADDED Egypt to the dominions of the Roman people',
says Augustus in the famous record of his career
known as the *Res Gestae*. The statement has been disputed by some modern writers, who have argued that
Egypt was never in any true sense a Roman province but
the private property of the Emperor. This view is not
really defensible. Egypt was indeed a province; but it
was a province of a peculiar kind. In form, under the
settlement of the year 27 B.C., the government of the
Roman Empire was (to use a term fashionable to-day) a
dyarchy: Augustus was not an autocratic emperor but
merely *princeps civitatis*, the first citizen in a free republic.
Authority over the provinces was divided between him
and the Senate. Those assigned to the latter were administered, as of old, by proconsular or propraetorian
governors subject to the Senate, the rest by the legates of
Caesar, drawn from the senatorial class.

Such was the form of the new order; the substance was
somewhat different. It is inexact to say, as has often been
asserted, that the provinces which required a military
garrison were assigned to Augustus, those which did not
to the Senate, for we hear of senatorial governors in
command of armies, but broadly speaking the statement
expresses the facts; and moreover Augustus enjoyed
maius imperium, an overriding authority, over the whole
Empire, which enabled him to interfere on occasion even
in senatorial provinces. In effect he monopolized
military power. It was the sword which had won him his
position; it was, ultimately, the sword which maintained

it. That, and the consent of the governed. It is possible, no doubt, to establish a dictatorship against the will of a large majority of the citizens, but unless their opposition can be converted into consent the government has no chance of permanence. And whatever resentments the Roman nobility, to whom the moribund republic had offered opportunities of wealth and aggrandizement now denied them, might cherish, there can be no doubt that by the Empire as a whole, wearied and exhausted by decades of civil war, the Augustan settlement was hailed with relief, by many even with enthusiasm. If, however, Caesar was to retain this goodwill he must fulfil two conditions: internal peace and order must be preserved, and the food-supply of Italy and the capital must be guaranteed. The chief granaries of the Empire were Africa and Egypt. Africa was a senatorial province, long pacified and requiring no great military force, but Egypt, recently conquered and with a reputation for turbulence, needed a strong garrison. Augustus placed there no less than three legions, with their quota of auxiliary troops—an unnecessarily large force, as his successor Tiberius decided when he withdrew one of the legions. As already said, Egypt is a highly defensible country. An ambitious commander, maintaining himself there, could hold up the corn-supply of Rome and at the same time cut one of the main commercial routes between the Empire and the East. Augustus decided that it would be unsafe to put such opportunities into the hands of a senator, and he therefore governed the country not through a senatorial legate but through a prefect of equestrian rank. Only in Egypt, nowhere else in the Empire, do we find a simple knight in command of a legionary army. Furthermore, he laid it down as one of those *arcana imperii*, those state secrets, which he confided to Tiberius, that no senator or *eques illustris* should be allowed to enter the country without the Emperor's express permission.

However, though Augustus was careful to bear himself at Rome as merely the first citizen, in Egypt he was the successor of the Ptolemies. To the Egyptians he was Pharaoh, 'Lord of the Two Lands', represented on the monuments with the usual divine attributes. The prefect, his viceroy, was subject to the taboo which forbade a king of Egypt to sail on the Nile during the inundation; the domain land continued to be known as royal land, each nome to have its royal secretary. Egypt was a province, but a province of a character unique in the Empire.

Though the country seems to have stood solidly behind Cleopatra, the royal authority had certainly been weak during much of the last century of Ptolemaic rule, and at times the Thebaid had been virtually independent. The first task for Rome was to establish order and a strong government. Augustus, as already said, assigned to Egypt a military force more than adequate, based on Alexandria but with detachments at various points up the Nile valley. Supreme authority was vested in the prefect, who was at once commander-in-chief of the army, head of the civil administration, chief financial officer, and (apart from a limited jurisdiction granted, in special cases, to certain of the central officials)[1] the sole dispenser of justice in Egypt. The administration of justice was indeed highly centralized: the old itinerant courts were replaced by the *conventus* or assize held periodically by the prefect, at Pelusium for the nomes of the eastern Delta, at Alexandria for those of the western Delta, and at Memphis for the rest of Egypt. The inconvenience which this must have entailed for litigants was to some extent obviated partly by the regular practice of delegation to local or other officials, partly through tours of inspection by the prefect, which made it possible on occasion to hold the *conventus* for Upper and Middle Egypt at places up the Nile valley. The business of the *conventus* was not confined to the trial of lawsuits and similar proceedings but included also a general submission and examination of the reports and accounts of the nome officials.

Among the greater central officials were the Juridicus, always a Roman knight, whose functions are not wholly clear but may possibly have included some of those exercised by a modern Minister of Justice, the Archidicastês, another judicial officer who might perhaps be compared, in virtue of his authority over the Public Record Office, with our Master of the Rolls, and the *Idios Logos* or procurator of the Special Account, responsible for all irregular or sporadic sources of revenue, like fines, confiscations, and acquisitions of unclaimed property.

Another important officer was the 'High Priest of Alexandria and all Egypt', who, though not himself a priest but a Roman civil official, was the supreme authority over all the temples and controlled the details of cult and temple organization. Through him Rome kept a tight hold on the priesthood, always the mouthpiece of Egyptian nationalism. The priests were required to submit to the *stratêgos* of the nome each year a return of personnel and property, along with the temple accounts. The temples were periodically inspected, the number of priests for each temple was fixed, and all in excess of that figure were subjected to the poll-tax, from which, in Ptolemaic times, the priesthood had been exempted. On the other hand, the Church, if we may use the term in this connexion, was guaranteed in the enjoyment of its restricted rights and privileges, and it was not till long after the conquest that we hear of any active opposition by priests to Roman rule.

In later Ptolemaic times the central government, in order the better to control the Thebaid, had established there an official known as an *epistratêgos* with ample powers, both civil and military. Augustus, taking the hint, divided Egypt into three large districts with an *epistratêgos* at the head of each. The three districts were the Thebaid, Middle Egypt (called officially 'the Seven Nomes and the Arsinoite nome'), and the Delta. The *epistratêgoi*, who were always Roman citizens, had no military power and seem to have been little concerned in financial matters; their functions were purely administrative and included the nomination of local officials.

It is probable, though some scholars take a contrary view, that Alexandria had lost the senate which it presumably possessed at its foundation before the end of the Ptolemaic period. Augustus certainly refused a request for the grant or restoration of a senate. If he refused it to Alexandria he was not likely to establish anything of the kind in the nome-capitals, which, though often towns of considerable size, remained, from a strictly constitutional point of view, no more than overgrown villages. His policy did, however, entail a certain advance in their status. It was based on that system of stratification into somewhat rigid classes of which the Romans were so fond. It was at one time universally believed that the racial policy ascribed to the Ptolemies, relaxed in the later days of the dynasty, was reasserted in an even stricter form by the Romans. We have seen that this conception requires modification as regards Ptolemaic

Egypt; it seems equally necessary to revise it for the Roman period. The old view was that a sharp distinction was made by the Roman government between Greeks, including the racially mixed but Hellenized inhabitants of the nome-capitals, and Egyptians, who were regarded as, in the Roman phraseology, *dediticii*, people of inferior status without any definite citizenship, and subject, as a mark of their inferiority, to a poll-tax. This theory has been called in question by Dr. Bickermann, whose arguments, though not universally accepted, seem to me convincing.[2] According to him, all inhabitants of Egypt were to the Romans 'Egyptians', with the exception of Roman citizens, the citizens of the three Greek self-governing cities, and very likely, though not certainly, the *katoikoi* or descendants of the military settlers in the Fayyûm. His view is supported by the evidence relating to the poll-tax. A tax of this kind had certainly existed under the Ptolemies, though its exact nature and incidence are somewhat obscure; the Roman tax, about which we are much better informed, seems to have been an adaptation of the older one. It was a money tax levied at a flat rate, without regard to income, on all those subject to it.[3] The *katoikoi* of the Fayyûm were probably exempt, as were certainly Romans, the citizens of the Greek cities, though not the Alexandrian Jews, and a fixed number of priests in each temple; everybody else was called on to pay the tax. A distinction was, however, made: the country population were assessed to the full amount, the metropolites of the nome-capitals paid at a reduced rate, which was perhaps everywhere, and was certainly in the Fayyûm, half the standard rate. These metropolites, however, did not include all the inhabitants of a nome-capital; they were a privileged class, presumably defined by Augustus in accordance with the degree of wealth and social standing, and in later times claiming the privilege in virtue of descent from the original holders. The intention is clear: it was to emphasize the superiority of Hellenic culture, to make a distinction between an urban and Hellenized *élite* and the mass of the peasantry. Even within the body of metropolites, though all paid the same reduced poll-tax, there was a distinction, an *élite* within an *élite*, a group known as *hoi apo gumnasiou*, 'the gymnasium class'. These were the wealthier residents, educated in the gymnasium, passing through the ephebate, and alone qualified for the urban magistracies.

These magistracies were another Roman innovation. The gymnasium was as characteristic a feature of Greek life as the club and the cricket-field of English, and wherever Greeks settled in organized communities a gymnasium would be established. It was the centre of higher education, alike physical and intellectual, and was closely associated with the ephebate, which was for a Greek youth the essential qualification for enrolment in the citizen body or in the *politeuma*, that social-political organization which for so many of the Greek settlers in Egypt replaced the city-state. Under the Ptolemies there were gymnasia, even in villages, wherever there was a sufficient body of Greek settlers, but these were private institutions. Augustus, who seems to have abolished the village gymnasia, gave to those in the nome-capitals an official status, as he did also to the gymnasiarch, the head of the gymnasium. At his side he established other urban magistrates, with titles and functions borrowed from the Greek city-states, the *exêgêtês* with various administrative functions, particularly concerned with questions of status, the *cosmêtês*, who was responsible for all matters affecting the ephebate, the high priest, controlling religious affairs, the *hypom-nématographos* or Recorder, the *agoranomos* or Superintendent of the Market, with special charge of the notariate, and the eutheniarch, whose sphere was the food-supply. At first these were individual magistrates, each responsible only for his own department, but in the course of time, certainly before the end of the second century A.D., they came to form a *koinon* or corporation, and thus provided the nucleus for the senates established by Septimius Severus. There was also in the nome-capitals some kind of general assembly of the citizens.⁴ Thus although these towns were neither cities in the Greek nor *municipia* in the Roman sense, they acquired under the Romans the semblance of municipal government.

There had been some kind of enrolment under the Ptolemies. The Romans introduced a regular census, taken every fourteen years and known as 'the house to house registration'. It was a census of house property as well as of persons; in some nomes the owner, in others the occupier, of every house was required to make under oath a return of his house and all its occupants, of every age and condition, to a commission appointed for the purpose. On the basis of these returns census rolls were compiled which contained a complete register of all the inhabitants. Returns of deaths and births helped to keep them in some degree up to date between the census years.⁵ Enrolment in a privileged class was secured by an examination, *epicrisis*, of the applicant's credentials, on a return made, usually by his parents, when he reached the age of fourteen (the time when liability to poll-tax began), submitting proof of his descent from privileged ancestors.

In addition to the central record offices at Alexandria

the Romans also established official repositories in every nome-capital. These institutions were later, at varying dates in different nomes, divided into two, the *bibliothêkê dêmosiôn logôn* or Public Record Office, which took charge of all official papers, such as correspondence, tax-rolls, land registers, census lists, and the like, and the *bibliothêkê enktêseôn* or Register of Real Property, including slaves. The returns and other documents sent in to these institutions were pasted together to form composite rolls, and other rolls were prepared containing abstracts and registers of the single documents. These rolls were often arranged in alphabetical order by the initials of the persons concerned, and reference to them was further facilitated by numbering the columns.[6]

For the rest, the general picture remained as under the Ptolemies. The old division of Egypt into nomes was maintained, each administered by a *stratêgos*, now shorn of all his military functions, and a royal secretary. The best land continued for the most part to form the royal domain and to bear the name royal land. The sacred land still figured in the land registers, though a good deal of it was confiscated at the conquest, and the temples were placed under stricter control than they had known in the later Ptolemaic age. To the gift-lands of Ptolemaic times corresponded certain great estates or *ousiai* acquired during the early Principate by members of the Imperial family and of the Roman and Alexandrian nobility. One by one, through confiscation or in other ways, these were absorbed into the Imperial *patrimonium* or private estate and thenceforward formed a special class of land called usiac land, controlled by an Imperial procurator. The cleruchic land still formed a separate category, though the military tenure ceased, and now at last became the full property of its owners.

Private property in land was indeed actively forwarded by the Romans, who liked to base their financial and administrative system on a population possessed of tangible assets which could guarantee the discharge of their liabilities or be drawn upon to compensate any default. A good deal of land had been confiscated after the conquest, and some of this was sold by auction, while derelict or inferior land was offered on terms favourable enough to tempt bidders to undertake its cultivation.

This, then, was the general pattern of Roman Egypt: a strong, centralized, and well-articulated administration, supported by a military force large enough to guarantee internal order and give security against marauding raids by desert nomads; an elaborate bureaucracy with an extended system of registers and controls; a social hierarchy based on caste and privilege; and a favoured treatment for the Hellenized population of the towns over the rural and native Egyptian populace.

When a strong, efficient, and reasonably honest administration replaces a weak and corrupt one there is bound to be an immediate increase in prosperity. Whatever may have been the state of Egypt under Cleopatra, the government during much of the later Ptolemaic period had certainly been nerveless and inefficient. Constant civil wars had devastated large areas, trade and industry had been interrupted, and the irrigation system had suffered from neglect. Roman rule, after the suppression of a fierce revolt which broke out in the Thebaid on the appearance there of the Roman tax-collectors, brought internal peace and security against invasion. Foreign trade was greatly stimulated by the incorporation of Egypt into the Roman Empire and particularly by the abolition of piracy in the Mediterranean, which was one of the chief benefits conferred by the Imperial régime, while the discovery of the monsoon, which appears to have occurred about the beginning of the Roman period,[7] led to a marked increase in the Indian and Eastern trade. Augustus set his army to the task of repairing and deepening the irrigation canals, with the result that, as Strabo informs us,[8] whereas before the conquest an abundant harvest required a rise of fourteen cubits in the level of the Nile and one of eight meant famine, under the Romans a rise of twelve brought a bumper harvest, and there was no scarcity even when it was only eight.

If, however, an efficient government is based on a vicious principle, its very efficiency may in the long run make it more harmful than a less competent one. So it proved now. No student of history can withhold a tribute of admiration from the Italian city-state which established an empire wider, more enduring, and better administered than any the Mediterranean world had previously known, and which for several centuries secured throughout its dominions an ease of communication and a unity of culture not to be seen again till modern times. We ourselves must be for ever grateful to the power which civilized western Europe and founded there a tradition of public order and municipal government destined to outlast the Empire itself and to be the seed of our civil liberties. In the East, however, where Rome came into contact with an older and finer civilization, she was less successful. The story of Roman Egypt at all events is a sad record of short-sighted exploitation leading inevitably to economic and social decline. I have already pointed out the fallacy of treating a nation as a mere estate, to be exploited for the benefit of the rulers. However incompetently some of the later Ptolemies might manage their estate, at least much of the wealth which they derived from it remained in the country itself, but Rome was an absentee landlord, and a large part of the corn delivered as rent by the royal tenants or as tax by landowners, as well as the numerous money-taxes, was sent to Rome, for the benefit of the Roman people, and represented a dead loss to Egypt. It was not that the Roman rulers had any evil intention. Warnings were frequently given against extortion— Tiberius, when a prefect sent him more than the statutory quota of taxes for the year, is reported to have reprimanded him, reminding him that he was sent to shear, not to flay, the sheep—and we have occasional evidence in the papyri of a fairly humanitarian attitude in individual cases;[9] but good intentions were useless so long as the root conception was maintained that Egypt was a cow to be milked for the benefit of Rome. The cow was no doubt rich in milk, but Rome systematically overmilked her. We need only read the so-called Gnomon or rules of the *Idios Logos* preserved in a papyrus at Berlin, or study the regulations for the leasing of domain lands or the collection of taxes, to recognize in them all the spirit of a rack-renting landlord or a sweating employer. Every crisis, every new difficulty, was met not by that radical reconstruction of the system which alone could have offered a remedy but by temporary measures of relief and a further extension of compulsion. It was always the fiscal interest that came first: nothing must be done, no concession must be made, which might endanger that. And the victims of the system knew this only too well, realized to what motive they could most safely appeal. In the last resort the working of the machine depended on them: if the liturgist defaulted, if the overburdened peasant left his holding, the fiscal interest would suffer; and so it was the threat of a refusal to co-operate which was their trump card, with this threat that petitions to the authorities regularly conclude. This note is heard as early as the reign of Nero: 'There is therefore a risk that owing to financial disability we may have to abandon the collectorship' declare the poll-tax collectors of some Fayyûm villages;[10] and in A.D. 180 a woman wrongly conscribed for a liturgy, using the now well-established technique, declares that she is 'in danger for this reason of having to leave my place of residence'.[11]

Even before the middle of the first century A.D. there were ominous signs. The Jewish philosopher Philo, writing in the reigns of Caligula and Claudius, gives a striking picture of contemporary conditions. He speaks of tax-collectors who would even seize the mummy of a defaulting taxpayer in order to coerce his relatives into payment of the arrears, of wives, children, and other relatives imprisoned and tortured in order to discover from them the whereabouts of a fugitive, of whole villages and even cities deserted by their inhabitants.[12] So long as we had no confirmatory evidence it was permissible to regard this as rhetorical exaggeration, but records found in Egypt have brought us proof that there is substantial truth in Philo's statements. So early as A.D. 20 we hear of the flight (*anachôrésis*) of taxpayers,[13] and in a papyrus written at some date between 55 and 60 the collectors of poll-tax from six villages in the Arsinoite nome report that 'the population in the foregoing villages, once numerous, has now shrunk to a few persons, because some have fled, having no means, and some have died without leaving relatives'.[14] This evidence does not stand alone. We have also the testimony of an edict issued by Tiberius Julius Alexander, the nephew of Philo, who, forsaking Judaism, became an officer in the

Roman army and from 66 to 70 was Prefect of Egypt.
It is true that this edict may, as has been suggested, have
had a propagandist purpose, in the interests of the party
opposed to Nero, and if so the prefect, who was a sup-
porter of Vespasian,[15] would not minimize the existing
evils; but the abuses referred to, the representations he
speaks of as made to him, and the remedies promised
are so specific as to leave no doubt that the document
provides authentic evidence of grave and far-reaching
irregularities. We hear of people compelled against
their will to undertake the farming of taxes and leases of
land (the latter statement is fully confirmed by papyrus
evidence), of the activity of informers who denounced
defaulters to the *Idios Logos*, of peasants, throughout the
whole country, burdened with new and irregular assessments.[16]

The measures of Tiberius Julius Alexander seem to
have borne fruit, for it is probably not owing merely to
accident that surviving records from the second half of
the first century contain fewer indications of serious
trouble. But already there had been introduced an
administrative innovation which was to prove disastrous.
The Ptolemaic bureaucracy had been mainly a profes-
sional one, recruited voluntarily. The collection of
taxes had been farmed out to tax-farmers, who made
their bids freely. The royal tenants, though restricted in
their liberty of movement, tendered voluntary applica-
tions for leases. In time of crisis the government was
indeed prepared to enrol qualified persons as officials
even against their will, to compel tax-farmers to undertake contracts and peasants to accept leases; but these
were exceptional cases. At first the Romans continued
the Ptolemaic practice, but gradually, in the course of
the first century A.D., a new principle was introduced,

that of the so-called liturgy, a term taken over from the Greek city-states, where the wealthier citizens were compelled to undertake such public services as the provision of choruses in the dramatic festivals and the equipment of warships. In Egypt this system, which, beginning with the smaller local offices, was gradually applied higher and higher up the administrative hierarchy, took the form of compelling qualified persons to assume certain public functions, like those of village elders, village secretaries, guards, financial officials, and (as direct collection replaced farming for the majority of taxes) tax-collectors. Probably the liturgists received some salary,[17] though our information on the point is very unsatisfactory, but this is not likely to have been adequate to the costs involved, and moreover they were responsible with person and property for all losses and deficiencies. The liturgical system, spreading like a cancer through the whole administrative structure short of the very highest posts, extending eventually even to the municipal magistracies, which in theory were voluntary and coveted distinctions (*honores*, as opposed to the liturgies, *munera*), and administered with an uncompromising rigidity, ended by ruining first the better-to-do peasantry and then the wealthier middle class.[18] Nor was compulsion confined to this sphere. So illiberal were the terms offered to the tenants of domain lands, so grudging the concessions made in times of economic stringency, that it was not infrequently impossible to find voluntary bidders. In such cases recourse was had to compulsion. One method was to assign unlet land in one village area to another village, where responsibility for its cultivation was distributed by lot among the villagers; another was that of the so-called *epibolé*, by which parcels of domain land were attached to land in private ownership, the owners being compelled to cultivate them along with their own holdings. By this means the domain land eventually, in the Byzantine period, almost disappeared, becoming merged in the private land with which it had been associated.[19] Under the first method, *epimerismos*, a whole community was held responsible for the cultivation and consequently (which was the main consideration) for the payment of the taxes; under the second the liability was individual. But as Philo indicates, and increasingly as time went on, a communal responsibility came to be assumed: if a taxpayer fled his taxes were charged to other members of the community, if a tenant or landowner defaulted or disappeared the duty of cultivating his land was assigned to others. Moreover, those whose duty it was to nominate office-holders, whether for *munera* or for *honores*, were regarded as guarantors and were themselves held to account on any default by their nominees. More and more as the years passed the individual must have felt himself enclosed in a net whose meshes were too fine to allow of any escape.

The full effects of the system were not apparent at first. On the whole the evidence points to a reasonable measure of prosperity in most of Egypt during the first century; such signs of acute crisis as I have mentioned were probably temporary or local. Even as regards the second century, during which the picture gradually darkens, there has been a tendency on the part of some writers to exaggerate its gloom. During the earlier part of the century a succession of able and enlightened emperors, among whom Hadrian was specially noteworthy for his sympathy with the provincials, secured a reasonably high standard of efficiency and equity in the administration. Archaeological evidence, as at Karanis in the Fayyûm, systematically excavated by the University of Michigan, does not reveal any marked deterioration in the standard of building or the amenities of social life before about the end of the century. The semi-municipal activity of the nome-capitals showed considerable vigour, and the tradition of Hellenic culture was well maintained. Discoveries at Oxyrhynchus, a mere nome-capital, not a Greek foundation, have shown that an astonishing range and variety of Greek classical literature was there available for study. Homer, as the main schoolbook in Greek education, was of course ubiquitous, nor need we wonder at the presence of Hesiod, but it is more surprising to find, in addition to the works which survived the Middle Ages and such authors as Sappho, Menander, and Callimachus, then mostly lost but familiar to readers throughout the earlier centuries of the Christian era, many works which some modern writers had too hastily assumed to have passed out of general currency by this time, among them fragments of many early lyric or iambic writers, of the Paeans and other poems of Pindar and his contemporaries, of lost plays of Aeschylus (nearly forty of whose dramas can be traced), besides others of Sophocles, Euripides, and Aristophanes, and specimens of meliambic and choliambic poetry. It is clear that the dweller at Oxyrhynchus, and so presumably other places in Egypt, had access to a vast body of literature, of which only a small portion now survives. There must have been a fairly large reading public and an active book-trade. An interesting papyrus letter not long since published[20] gives us a vivid glimpse into a bookish circle at Oxyrhynchus. 'Make and send me copies of books 6 and 7 of Hypsicratês' *Characters in Comedy.* For Harpocratiôn says that they are among Pôliôn's books. But it is likely that others, too, have got them. He also has prose epitomes

of Thersagoras' work on the myths of tragedy.' So
the writer of the letter; another hand adds: 'According to Harpocratiôn Demetrius the bookseller has got
them.'

Though illiteracy was common, especially among
women, education was by no means confined to a
wealthy *élite* but was widely valued and pursued in that
middle class which Roman policy had done so much to
create. Beginning with instruction in reading and
writing, first the alphabet, then single syllables of two,
three, or more letters, then whole words, sometimes
written syllable by syllable,[21] the curriculum proceeded
by stages to the study of grammar, rhetoric, literature,
mathematics (including mensuration), and philosophy.
The pupils were required to write compositions and at a
later stage to compose speeches on set themes. They were
taught something of Greek legend and mythology, and
the frequent choice of gnomic sentences for reading
exercises shows a bias in the direction of moral instruction, though some of these *gnômai* are of a rather cynical
kind, like the epigrams attributed to Simonides. Homer,
provided the foundation of the whole educational
system: 'I took care to send and inquire about your
health and to learn what you were reading. He [the
teacher] said it was the 6th book', writes a mother to her
son; it was unnecessary to specify that the book was a
book of the *Iliad*.[22] The dramatists, both tragic and
comic, the chief lyric poets, and, of course, the orators
were also studied. In at least the elementary stages,
much use was made, for educational purposes, of potsherds or ostraca and of waxed tablets, which could be
employed again and again. Naturally text-books were
needed: 'I beg of you to [ask?] my guardian to assign me
the necessaries for school, such as a reading book for

Hêraidous', writes a schoolboy of the early second century.[23] Since Hêraidous was a girl, the daughter of a *stratêgos*, this letter points to a practice of co-education. It has been suggested[24] that many of the papyri in which a literary text was written on the verso of a roll previously used for an official document may have been school copies. Besides the local schools and the education imparted in the gymnasia there appear to have been teachers of standing who took pupils from a distance, anticipating in some degree the modern boarding-school. When schooldays were passed those desirous of higher education could get it in the University of Alexandria. A recently published letter[25] from a student, probably in that city, illustrates vividly the mentality of an ancient undergraduate. Unfortunately, though understandably enough, he tells us nothing of his course of study; and we need not take too seriously his verdict on the teaching: 'As for myself, if only I had found some decent teachers, I would pray never to set eyes on Didymus, even from a distance—what makes me despair is that this fellow who used to be a mere provincial teacher sees fit to compare with the rest. However, knowing as I do that apart from paying useless and excessive fees there is no good to be had from a teacher, I'm depending on myself.' Instruction in special subjects, like shorthand, which was in request for the law-courts and administrative offices, seems to have been given by way of apprenticeship.[26]

This typically Greek education naturally included, as a very important element, physical training, the sports of the palaestra and the semi-military exercises of the ephebes. Ephebic displays and other public celebrations, on the occasion of a religious festival, the accession of an emperor, or an Imperial birthday, provided enjoyable spectacles for the inhabitants of the nome-capitals. There were periodic games, at which athletes of various classes competed in boxing,[27] wrestling, running, and the like. There were certainly dramatic performances. It is reasonable to suppose that inhabitants of a metropolis had occasional opportunities of seeing the classical works of Greek tragedy and the New Comedy; they certainly could enjoy popular farces and mimes presented at the local theatre or music-hall.[28] And itinerant parties of musicians, dancers, tumblers, and the like catered for the entertainment of villagers in the remoter parts of the nomes.[29] Life in second-century Egypt was certainly not without its amenities. Nor, despite the net of regulations and restrictions which enmeshed them, did the workers wholly lack means of making their grievances known: 'All our people', writes a woman of the wealthy class from Hermopolis to her daughter in the reign of Trajan, 'have been in procession all round the town, demanding higher wages.'[30]

Notwithstanding the common custom of exposing unwanted infants, a practice which, since it was economic in origin, was probably confined in the main to the poorer classes, the papyri give us plenty of glimpses into happy family life, birthday celebrations, dinner parties, and other social functions, the purchase of toys and sweetmeats for the children, and private letters warm with family affection.

Nevertheless, as I have said, economic prosperity was being gradually undermined. By the beginning of the second century the liturgical principle was fully established for all state offices or *munera*, as they were called in Latin, except the highest, and was already beginning to invade the sphere of the urban magistracies, the *honores*. In A.D. 115 the gymnasiarchy at Hermopolis was still

normally voluntary,[31] but when in 130 Hadrian founded
the new Greek city of Antinoopolis in memory of his
favourite Antinous, drawing the citizens from various
nomes, he gave them, among other special privileges,
that of exemption from liability to both *munera* and
honores outside their own city.[32] In the following reign,
that of Antoninus Pius, a decree of the Oxyrhynchites in
honour of a townsman stresses the fact that he had
voluntarily undertaken the gymnasiarchy.[33] Before the
end of the century compulsion had become the normal
and indeed invariable practice,[34] and so far was the
voluntary principle disappearing from consciousness
that in the third century we find the word *liturgy* used of
both *munera* and *honores*. From the year 202 we have a
papyrus in which a wealthy Alexandrine asks Imperial
permission to found a charitable trust for the support of
liturgists in certain villages of the Oxyrhynchite nome
which, owing to 'the burdensome demands of the annual
liturgies', were 'in danger of being ruined so far as the
Treasury is concerned and of leaving your land uncultivated'.[35] It was becoming ever more difficult to
find suitable candidates for the urban magistracies.
Several papyri record infringements of the immunity
conferred by Hadrian on the Antinoopolites, and the
overburdened metropolites were even attempting to
force the inhabitants of villages into urban magistracies,
a practice which had to be forbidden by Septimius
Severus. As there were now few persons able to support
these burdensome charges for a whole year the single
magistrates were replaced by boards, each member of
which exercised the functions of the office in rotation.
In the later third century we find gymnasiarchs, for
example, acting for a few days only.

By this date we have to reckon with a new factor,

Christianity. On the early diffusion of Christianity in Egypt we are singularly ill informed.[36] The tradition that the Alexandrian Church was founded by St. Mark may probably be dismissed as a legend, but it can be assumed that the new faith would not be long in reaching the chief port in the eastern Mediterranean, and once there it was bound to spread to other parts of Egypt. Yet it has left no trace in any of the first-century papyri so far discovered, and even in documents of the second century there is remarkably little clear evidence of its influence. That it was already well established in Middle and Upper Egypt may, however, be inferred from the evidence of literary papyri. We have now fragments of no less than seven Biblical papyri which can with confidence be assigned to the second century, one of them, a small scrap of St. John's Gospel, dated by all competent authorities quite early in the period.[37] For every such papyrus which accident has preserved there must have been hundreds which have perished, for every Christian who owned such a papyrus scores who did not.

The rarity of references in our papyrus documents to the Christian faith may be attributed in part to the necessity for concealing any connexion with a persecuted sect, but this need not be taken as the sole cause: legal contracts and returns to officials did not call for any mention of Christianity, and private letters, largely couched in stereotyped and conventional phrases and usually concerned with severely practical matters, might be equally neutral. It is as mistaken to suppose that persecution was unbroken as it is to think that the persecutions of Christians carried out by the Roman government were directed against their religious beliefs as such. Rome was very tolerant in matters of religion;

when she tried to suppress any cult it was primarily on moral or political grounds. To the authorities Christians were bad citizens and a dangerous element in the community. They stood aloof from the rites of the official religion, they did not venerate the Imperial effigies or take part in the cult of Rome or the Genius of the Emperor, their solidarity and the privacy of their worship suggested a secret society, they were accused of monstrous practices. Incest, obscene rites, ritual murder—such were the charges brought by pagans against the Christians, as in later centuries they were to be brought by Christians against the Jews. But there were always pagans who would shelter Christian friends, and provincial governors were often extremely reluctant to enforce the penal laws. Only in times of public calamity or popular excitement was persecution general; as Tertullian says in a famous passage,[38] 'If the Tiber reaches the walls, if the Nile fails to reach the fields, if the heaven withholds its rain, if the earth quakes, if there is famine, if there is pestilence, at once the cry is raised "The Christians to the lion!" ' On such occasions there were some whose courage was unequal to the test, but there were also many who stood firm. It is impossible to read the earlier and more obviously authentic narratives of martyrdoms, like the Passion of St. Perpetua or the Acts of the Scillitan Martyrs, without being profoundly moved by the unostentatious but unflinching heroism displayed by both men and women, in particular perhaps, when we remember their context, by the simple words *Christianus* (or *Christiana*) *sum*, 'I am a Christian'.[39] They are words not always easily spoken even to-day, in a nominally Christian country, but in the second and third centuries they earned, not just a sneer or a mocking laugh from unsympathetic companions, but the prospect of such a death as might shake the constancy of the bravest: the packed amphitheatre with its crowds avid for blood, the little group of Christians in the arena, the mauling by lion or leopard on the blood-stained sand, and in the end the merciful sword which brought relief to the mangled body. From the middle of the third century we have a group of papyri which illustrate vividly the persecution of Decius. They are examples of those *libelli* or certificates of sacrifice to the pagan deities which the Emperor had ordered all subjects of the Empire to submit. Those who presented none were adjudged Christians; but some weaker members of the flock compromised with their conscience by sending in false certificates.[40]

Egyptian Christianity seems to have had a tendency to heretical opinions, particularly in the direction of gnosticism, a fact which probably accounts for the popularity in Egypt of St. John's Gospel, with its doctrine of the Logos and its strain of mysticism. It has indeed been suggested that this Gospel was written at Alexandria,[41] which would certainly help to explain the apparent ignorance of it shown by Polycarp.[42] Alexandria, which had suffered greatly from the civil wars and disturbances which had troubled Egypt during the later Ptolemaic period, and of which it had more than once been the centre, enjoyed a period of increased prosperity under Roman rule. It was the second city of the Empire and the greatest port in the Mediterranean, with an active trade, westwards and northwards to Italy and the western provinces, to Greece and Asia Minor, eastwards as far as to India. The city no longer, as in the third century B.C., harboured poets of high poetic rank, though it still had a school of poetry and imaginative literature, but distinguished scholars and scientists, such as Ptolemy and Hêrôn, gave it lustre, and the Jewish community produced notable writers, like Philo. The university attracted students not only from Egypt but from across the sea.

Yet this prosperity did not reconcile the citizens to Roman rule. They had given their Macedonian kings plenty of trouble, but they resented the loss of Alexandria's position as a royal residence and the capital of an independent kingdom, and all through the Roman period, though individual emperors, like Gaius (Caligula) and Nero, had a great partiality for the city, the citizens carried on an embittered feud with the Roman government. Since the Jews had been confirmed by Augustus in all their privileges, whereas he had refused the Alexandrines the senate they asked for, this feud often took the form of anti-Semitism: it was safer to attack the Jews than the Romans directly. Pogroms and faction fights were of frequent occurrence and often led to military action by the Roman garrison, to embassies sent by one or both sides to the Emperor (like that so vividly described by Philo in his *Legatio ad Gaium*), and to trials of prominent Alexandrines in the Imperial courts. A whole patriotic literature, called by modern scholars, owing to its resemblance to the Christian Acts of the Martyrs, *Acta Alexandrinorum* or 'Pagan Acts of the Martyrs', in which the courage and independence of the Alexandrian leaders were magnified, sprang up and enjoyed great popularity. These leaders are represented as treating Caesar with extraordinary boldness: 'You are the cast-off son of Salome, the Jewess', declares a gymnasiarch to Claudius,[43] and he refers contemptuously to the Emperor's friend Herod Agrippa as 'a twopenny-halfpenny Jew'.[44] The Alexandrines carried with them on one occasion a bust of their patron god Sarapis, which broke, we are told, into a miraculous sweat, to the consternation of the Romans.[45] The memory of their 'martyrs' was long cherished among the Alexandrines, as Christians venerated theirs.[46]

Just as in Ptolemaic times Alexandria had seen the translation of the Jewish scriptures into Greek for the use of a largely Hellenized Jewish community, just as in the first century A.D. Philo had formulated a Judaic philosophy in the Greek language and on the model of Greek philosophic speculation, so in the second and third centuries the city was a centre for a certain reconciliation between the best thought of paganism and the nascent intellectual world of Christianity. It is a remarkable fact that Anatolius, ordained Bishop of Laodicea in A.D. 269, should have been elected by the Alexandrines, whose fellow-citizen he was, to be the professor of Aristotelian philosophy at Alexandria.[47] And side by side with the Museum and its pagan learning flourished the great Christian Catechetical School founded by Pantaenus, the chief ornaments of which were St. Clement and Origen. A convert from paganism, the former was a man of wide erudition (which he was perhaps rather too fond of displaying) and took an important part in the process of wedding the religious experience of Christianity to Greek culture. Though an ardent and orthodox Christian and the upholder of a strict and even austere morality, he was essentially a humanist. He allows and indeed defends the use of wine; he does not wholly forbid some concession to the claims of beauty and comfort in social life; he retained even after his conversion his love of classical literature and his veneration for Plato; he had a real vein of humour and a gift of pungent satirical phrase; and his contemptuous reference to some of the pagan priests 'who never come near a bath and let their nails grow to an extraordinary length, like wild beasts'[48] shows a love of personal cleanliness which would sound strangely to those unwashed anchorites of a later day who, as a cynic has remarked, did in literal truth exemplify the 'odour of sanctity'.[49] Origen, though he lacked Clement's extensive acquaintance with Greek literature, was endowed with a profounder intellect, a better grasp of philosophical principles, a finer sense of scholarship, and a more original mind; indeed he ranks among the greatest figures of the Christian Church. Finally, just as Alexandria had produced a lasting effect on the texts of classical authors, so at this later date it made very important contributions to the task of establishing a trustworthy text of the New Testament. The exact nature and extent of these contributions are still subjects of controversy, but they were certainly considerable; and if it was at Caesarea, not Alexandria, that Origen completed that imposing monument of scholarship, the *Hexapla*, it was at Alexandria, of which he was a native, that he began it, there that he had acquired the knowledge to carry it out.

A striking change in the status of the nome-capitals was made in the year 202, when Septimius Severus established senates or municipal councils. At the same time Alexandria saw the fulfilment of a long-cherished wish by the receipt of a similar body, though the gift must have lost some of its attractiveness through the knowledge that it was shared by the nome-capitals. In the latter the new measure did not even yet denote full municipal status. The *stratêgos* was still the chief administrator of the nome, and he had authority over the senate and the metropolis, where he continued to reside.

It was no more than a modified form of municipal self-government which had been received; and though it was doubtless represented, and was apparently accepted, as a privilege, it was in fact an added burden on the class, the wealthier townsmen, from whom the senate was recruited. That body was now responsible for the financial administration of the nome-capital; it had to appoint and therefore to warrant not only the urban but also many of the state officials, among them the newly introduced *dekaprôtoi*,[50] whose duty it was to superintend the collection and storage of the tax corn; it was charged with supervision of the temple finances. The responsibility was collective: each member of a college of magistrates, each senator was held liable not only for his own shortcomings but for those of his colleagues and of the body to which he belonged. Since it is likely that persons not previously on the rota of those liable to be charged with the magistracies were enrolled in the senate,[51] the financial burden was more widely spread, though not the less crushing for those who shared it. To refuse a magistracy or membership of the senate was possible only through the so-called *cessio bonorum*, the surrender of two-thirds of the nominee's property.[52] It is no exaggeration to say that the introduction of the senates was the decisive step in the ruin of the Hellenized *bourgeoisie*.

A further change occurred ten years later, when in 212 Caracalla, by the famous measure known as the *Constitutio Antoniniana*, conferred the Roman citizenship on all the inhabitants of the Empire. For the new citizens in Egypt the enhancement of status can have brought little, if any, advantage. They now became liable to the *vicesima hereditatum* or tax of one-twentieth on inheritances levied on Roman citizens, but without obtaining exemption from the Egyptian poll-tax. They were subject to the Roman civil law, but in fact the actual legal practice, as revealed in papyrus documents, was not so much changed as might have been expected. The Graeco-Egyptian law had already been influenced by Roman law; it now coloured the latter, and the papyri written after Caracalla show in fact a legal system by no means fully in harmony with the precepts of Roman jurists.

As the third century advanced signs of impending collapse multiplied,[53] despite a tendency to bombastic titles (like 'the illustrious and most illustrious city of the Oxyrhynchites') and extravagant schemes of town-planning on the part of the nome-capitals. It was more and more difficult to fill the urban magistracies. The number of nominations to each office was increased, the period of service shortened; Oxyrhynchus, as we learn from an official letter written about 289,[54] had for a considerable time previously had no eutheniarch at all. We hear frequently of flight or threats of flight by liturgists; compulsory leases of the domain lands were now regular; there is evidence of rural depopulation. A much mutilated papyrus in the British Museum provides striking testimony to the state of things in the middle of the century. It is a report of a trial before the prefect Appius Sabinus, probably in the first half of the year 250.[55] Despite the prohibition by Septimius Severus, the authorities at Arsinoê, the capital of the Fayyûm, were again attempting to force villagers into the municipal magistracies. The villagers resisted the claim, and the case came before the prefect. Their counsel produced the law of Severus, and the prefect asked the opposing counsel if they could cite an ordinance in the opposite sense. The reply by one of them was: 'The laws are indeed to be held in reverence, but you in trying the case must follow [the decisions?] of prefects who have had regard to the needs of the cities; it is the need of the city which limits the application of the law.' At a later stage of the trial the prefect again confronted the counsel of the metropolis with the law of Severus, and the answer was: 'To the law of Severus I will say this: Severus ordained the law in Egypt while the cities were still prosperous.' 'The argument from prosperity, or rather the decline in prosperity' (replied the prefect) 'applies equally to both the villages and the cities.' In other words, the economic crisis was universal. It was indeed an unhappy time for the whole Empire. There was constant civil war as one pretender after another arose to claim the Imperial purple. Few successful claimants maintained themselves on the throne for as much as ten years, and the invariable end of a reign was a death by violence. Foreign was added to intestine war. The Teutonic barbarians broke through the northern ramparts of the Empire, and the Goths penetrated deep into Greece and sacked Athens. In the East the revived Persian Empire of the Sassanids was a constant menace, and the Emperor Valerian was himself taken prisoner by a Persian army. Pestilence carried off tens of thousands of victims; land was everywhere going out of cultivation; constant depreciations of the currency led to inflation and a dizzy rise in prices. It was the supreme crisis of the Empire, and it seemed that the Roman power was in its death agony.

I have said that the *Constitutio Antoniniana* did not abolish poll-tax. This is clear; but it is equally clear that poll-tax played little part in the economy of third-century Egypt. After the middle of the century there are no direct references to it whatever, and even before

that such references are very rare in documents later
than Caracalla. Poll-tax, like others of the innumerable
taxes so prominent in papyri of the first and second
centuries, was being replaced by new sources of revenue.
One of these was the crown tax, originally nominally a
free-will offering to a ruler on his accession but later
becoming, like the Benevolences of Edward IV and
other English kings, a compulsory levy which was eventually made annual. It was a money tax, payable on
landed property, and probably, unlike the poll-tax,
which was levied at a fixed rate, it could be varied to
suit the needs of the moment.[56] Even more effective
was the *annona militaris*. This was properly a requisi-
tioning of supplies for the army, which now received an
increasing proportion of its pay in kind. Requisitions
could be made as and when required, and to the extent
called for by momentary exigencies, an arrangement
very burdensome to the taxpayer but convenient for the
financial authorities, who were responsible with person
and property for the full quota of taxes. Money was
losing its value; the rate of poll-tax had not been increased proportionately to the reduced purchasing
power of the coinage; and overburdened taxpayers
were apt to disappear when their position became
desperate. Supplies in kind were doubtless easier to
trace and secure; moreover, the *annona* was a communal
levy, not an individual capitation charge like the poll-
tax, and if one taxpayer defaulted those who remained
could be more readily drawn on than in the case of a
money tax. It must be added that cash could be
accepted in lieu of supplies in kind if expedient. Receipts for *annona* begin to appear among our papyri in
the reign of Septimius Severus, and grow ever commoner throughout the third century.

Even in a time of general economic decay there are usually enterprising men who, if backed by sufficient capital, can make their profit out of the prevailing conditions by adapting their methods of exploitation to the changed circumstances.[57] So it was now. We have from the middle of the third century an interesting collection of documents known as the Hêrôninus papyri.[58] They were the papers of a man so named, who was the steward or bailiff of some large estates at Theadelphia in the Fayyûm. His principal employer was a certain Alypius, who perhaps held no official position but is once referred to by an honorific title corresponding to the Latin *vir egregius*, a man therefore of rank and importance. Others were Appianus, a former *exêgêtês* of Alexandria, and Hêraclidês, a senator and ex-gymnasiarch of Arsinoê. Alypius had a whole troop of servants, secretaries, stewards, and the like, and owned very extensive estates in various parts of the Fayyûm. It is a matter of dispute whether he and his like were landowners or merely lessees of state lands. Personally I incline to the former view, but the point is not of great importance, for even if the lands were state property they were presumably assigned to their possessors on hereditary leases, one of the ways in which the domain land passed eventually into private ownership. Alypius in fact, there seems little doubt, was the forerunner of those great nobles, owning vast estates, whom we shall meet in the later Byzantine period. Already we see the beginning of a great agrarian revolution. The characteristic feature of rural Egypt in the Roman period was a rural community consisting on the one hand of comparatively small landowners, on the other of tenants of the domain lands. In the economy of the sixth century we shall find that the domain lands figure hardly at all, and the most salient impression we receive is of a country divided between a semi-feudal nobility and a half-servile peasantry. Probably it was in the third century that the process began which led to this result. The agony of the Empire finds scant echo in these Hêrôninus papers, which are occupied with more personal and immediate affairs.

'God willing, expect us', writes Alypius to Hêrôninus, 'to visit you on the 23rd. The moment you receive my letter, therefore, be sure to have the bathroom heated, having logs carried into it and collecting chaff wherever you can get it, so that we may have a hot bath this wintry weather. For we have decided to put up at your house, with the idea of both inspecting the remaining estates and arranging the work of your section. But mind you see to all our other requirements; above all, provide a good pig for our party, but see that it *is* a good one, not a lean useless thing like the last time. Send word also to the fishermen to bring us fish. . . . Have an ample quantity of green grass brought in, so that my working animals also may have plenty of food'.[59]

This letter and scores like it may usefully remind us that beneath and behind all the turmoil of war and revolution and the social and economic upheavals which the historian chronicles the rhythm of life goes on, the average man more concerned about his personal affairs, a business transaction, a family anniversary, to-morrow's dinner, than about distant battles or the evolving pattern of society.

> Only a man harrowing clods
> In a slow silent walk
> With an old horse that stumbles and nods
> Half asleep as they stalk.

Only thin smoke without flame
From the heaps of couch-grass;
Yet this will go onward the same
Though Dynasties pass.

In the autumn of 284 the army of the East chose as its candidate for the throne the commander of the household guards, Dioclês, or, as he called himself henceforward, Diocletian, who, on the death of Carinus, became Emperor. A Dalmatian of humble birth, he was a sound though not brilliant soldier, and a statesman of large views, fertile and ingenious mind, and sanguine temperament. The task which faced him was a formidable one, no less than to save the Empire from dissolution, but he lacked neither the courage nor the capacity for it. His reforms mark one of the great turning-points of history. Already the Principate, the overriding authority of the first citizen, had given place to the Dominate, the autocratic rule of a divine Emperor, but there still lingered some tenuous shadow of republican forms and at least the pretence of a division of powers between Emperor and Senate. With Diocletian we reach a fully developed absolutism and, though Byzantium did not become the capital of the Empire till the reign of Constantine the Great, we enter the Byzantine period. We are still in the ancient world, but already we feel some premonition of the Middle Ages.

Impressed by the magnitude of the Imperial burden, Diocletian decided to enlist the support of a colleague. As finally established, his system involved the simultaneous rule of two emperors holding the title of Augustus, and two coadjutors and heirs apparent with that of Caesar. Anxious to avoid the constant danger of disorder which arose from the ambitions of provincial governors possessed of both military and civil powers, and feeling perhaps that a governor's functions were too manifold for full efficiency, he reorganized the provinces. The distinction between senatorial and Imperial provinces was abolished; the provinces were reduced in size; and military were separated from civil powers. The single provinces were grouped into larger units known as dioceses (*dioikêseis*). Egypt, hitherto one province, became three, the Thebaid, Aegyptus Herculia, and Aegyptus Jovia, the two former each under a governor with the title of *praeses*, the latter, which included Alexandria, under the *praefectus Aegypti* or Prefect of Egypt, who had authority superior to that of the *praesides* but was himself, like them, subordinate to the Count of the Orient, to whose diocese Egypt belonged. All three were purely civil officials; military power was concentrated in the hands of the *Dux Aegypti* or Duke of Egypt.

Diocletian further undertook a drastic reorganization of the fiscal system. This he based on the principle of the *annona*, but he regularized and stabilized what had hitherto been special and unforeseeable levies. Every year there was drawn up an *indictio* or estimate of the requirements for the year, fixing the quota of each province, which was informed of the amount by means of the *delegatio*. The assessment, carried out at first every five years, later every fifteen, was founded on what might be called units of productivity. For landed property such a unit was called a *iugum*; it was the amount of cultivable land which could be worked by one man, and the size varied according to the quality of the land. Thus, in Syria the *iugum* consisted of twenty, forty, or sixty acres of plough-land, five acres of vineyard, or 225 (in mountainous districts 450) olive-trees. For human beings the unit was the *caput* or head, a woman being reckoned as half a *caput*.[60]

The result of these changes was a great simplification of the very complex system which characterized the Roman period, and the majority of the taxes familiar in earlier papyri now disappear from our documents. A papyrus happily discovered not long ago preserves for us the edict of the prefect Aristius Optatus announcing the reform:

'Our most provident Emperors Diocletian and Maximian, the Augusti, and Constantius and Maximian, the most noble Caesars, [having learned] that the assessments of the public revenues have come to be made in such a way that some persons are let off too lightly, while others are overburdened, have thought it good to root out this most evil and pernicious practice in the interests of their provincials, and to establish a salutary standard in accordance with which the tax-payments shall be made. I have therefore publicly displayed the amount imposed on each aroura in proportion to the quality of the land and on each head of the rural population, with the minimum and maximum ages of liability, in accordance with the divine edict which has been published and the brief annexed thereto.'[61]

Here we find both the *iugatio* and the *capitatio*, both the territorial and the personal units of productivity, provided for. We shall see in the next chapter what were the results of Diocletian's innovations.

IV

THE BYZANTINE PERIOD

THE reforms of Diocletian, described in the last
chapter, radically altered the administrative pattern of Egypt. The country now formed not one
province but three; there was a complete separation of
civil and military powers; and the taxation system and
the methods of assessment were organized on new lines.
In one respect, however, there was at first no change.
The old nome organization was retained, and the position of the nome-capitals still fell short of full municipal
status. The final step towards municipalization was
taken after Diocletian's abdication (1 May 305), at an
uncertain date between 307 and 310. By this measure
the nome ceased to be the unit of administration, and
with it disappeared the offices of *stratêgos* (at least in the
old form) and royal secretary. The senate was now
charged with full responsibility for both finance and
general administration. Egypt, from being a complex
of nomes, each with its nome-capital and administered
by a *stratêgos*, became a complex of self-governing
civitates or municipalities, each with its rural area, its
territorium or (in Greek) *enoria*. This territory, which
corresponded generally with the old nome (though
some rearrangements were made), was divided into
numbered *pagi* or cantons, equivalent to the former
subdivisions of the nome known as toparchies and com-
parable with our rural districts. Each *pagus* was
financially administered by a *praepositus* or provost,
subordinate to the *exactor*, a municipal official newly
created, to whom were transferred the financial duties

of the *stratêgos*, while the *propoliteuomenos* or chairman of the senate took over the other functions of the latter. The partial equivalence of the *exactor*'s tasks to those of the *stratêgos* led to his being known on occasion by that title, but this is a merely titular survival. Probably rather later but certainly before 336 was introduced another official, the *defensor*, whose primary function was to protect the poorer inhabitants against oppression by the richer, the *humiliores* against the *potentiores*.

The net result of these changes was a greater degree of assimilation to the other provinces of the Empire than Egypt had known previously, though geographical and other factors still involved a certain measure of difference. It was indeed a leading characteristic of Diocletian's policy to aim at a unification and simplification of the administrative system, and thereby to consolidate the forces of the Empire. To this desire was due another measure which has left its mark on our papyrus records, the introduction of Latin as the official language even in provinces where, as in Egypt, Greek had hitherto held that position. But the actual change was slight. Greek continued to be the main language of the law courts, of the administrative departments, and of public pronouncements. The main result of the new order visible in our records is that the official reports of law cases have now a Latin framework; that is to say, the heading, date, and connecting narrative are in that language, sometimes, too, the remarks of the prefect himself, while the speeches, alike of parties, witnesses and counsel, and often of the presiding judge, continue to be in Greek. A further change was the abandonment of the Emperor's regnal year in the dating clause of legal documents and the substitution of the consulship, with the indiction, that is to say, the year of

the fifteen year cycle between assessments.[1] This practice continued until the abolition of the consulship by
Justinian, after which regnal datings were reintroduced.
A further and welcome result of Diocletian's policy is
the survival of numerous Latin papyri from the Byzantine period, a knowledge of Latin having become a
desirable asset to those anxious to make a career for
themselves.

The desire for unification was no doubt one of the
motives for what is now the most widely known of Diocletian's measures, his persecution of the Christians.
The mortar which held together an empire embracing
many races and peoples differing in background,
speech, and culture, was the common observance of the
state religion. The Christians, refusing their participa-
tion in pagan rites, were an alien and unassimilated
element in the body politic, and it was natural therefore
that steps should be taken to absorb or eliminate them.
Yet it seems clear that the Great Persecution was not
due to Diocletian's own initiative. It was ordered by
him only with extreme reluctance, under strong pressure
from the Caesar Galerius, and on the express condition
that there should be no bloodshed. Fires in the Imperial palace, which happened as conveniently and as
suspiciously as the Reichstag fire, led to a sharpening of
the measures against the Christians, and later Galerius
took advantage of a dangerous illness which attacked
Diocletian to issue a new edict imposing the death
penalty. It has even been suggested that Diocletian's
abdication was not unconnected with his disapproval of
what was going on.[2] At all events battle was now
joined, and it was to be a battle to the death. Churches
were destroyed, scriptural and religious books were
burned, there were many martyrdoms. It was by so

much the greatest persecution yet suffered that the
Coptic Church of Egypt and Abyssinia still dates by the
Era of Diocletian or the Era of the Martyrs.

The blood of the martyrs is the seed of the Church,
Tertullian had said,[3] and it was true on this occasion
also. It is highly probable that in a world sick and
hungry for spiritual support every martyrdom won new
converts to a faith which could inspire such courage.
We must remember, too, that the Church celebrates not
only martyrs but confessors. A confessor is a man or
woman who, while ready to face the prospect of death,
did not actually suffer the extreme penalty. Hundreds
died, but there were thousands who were merely imprisoned or banished to remote parts of the Empire, and
they took with them their example and their zeal for
making converts. Thus the very measure designed to
eradicate the 'plague' of Christianity only spread the
contagion more widely. To judge from papyri Egypt
in 300, though it contained a very large number of
Christians, was still in the main a pagan country; by
330 it seems already to have been a predominantly
Christian one. This change was no doubt due in part
not to persecution but to its discontinuance. On the
30th April 311 Galerius, stricken with a loathsome
disease, called off the persecution and appealed to the
Christians for their prayers. The prayers were given,
but in vain, and Galerius died a few days later.

There was some persecution after this, but with Constantine and Maxentius in the West inclined to toleration it was sporadic and local. In 312 Constantine,
who had broken with Maxentius and was embarking
on war against him, saw the famous vision of which he
himself told the ecclesiastical historian Eusebius: a
cross against the sun with the words *hoc vince*, 'By this

prevail'. It is natural for a sceptic like Seeck to dismiss the story as 'of course a lie' and to attribute the change in Constantine's attitude to purely political motives; but the historian, however eminent, is a bold man who seeks to interpret the history of the fourth century on the lines of modern rationalism. There is no sufficient reason for doubting that Constantine believed he had had a revelation; and though political considerations may have suggested a policy of tolerance we are certainly not justified in assuming that he, who had been a devotee of the Unconquered Sun, was uninfluenced by religious ideas also. Certainly he was so confident of victory that with inadequate forces, against the advice of his generals and the forecasts of his augurs, he invaded Italy and made for the almost impregnable fortress of Rome; and it was with the cross on their shields that his troops marched to the Battle of the Milvian Bridge which gave him the mastery of the West.[4] In 313 he and his ally Licinius published the famous Edict of Milan which established the principle of religious toleration, and when in September 323 he defeated Licinius and found himself sole Emperor the way was clear for Christianity to become first the predominant and then the sole official religion of the Roman Empire.

'Ah Constantine! to how much ill gave birth, not thy conversion, but that dower which the first rich Father took from thee!' writes Dante.[5] The so-called donation of Constantine, to which he alludes, is a myth, but we may well feel that the consequences of the Emperor's conversion were not wholly good. It was now not merely safe but fashionable to be a Christian, and many time-servers hastened to espouse the winning cause. The Church, moreover, was free to indulge that tendency to theological disputation which had already troubled it even under persecution. The squabbles of the fourth and following centuries, with their fierce animosities, their personal ambitions and rivalries, the frequent unscrupulousness of their tactics, and their absence of elementary Christian charity, are not a pretty story. It is perhaps charitable to regard them as the growing pains of the Church, its laborious effort to give abstract and philosophical formulation to a religious experience based on the life and teaching of a personal Founder. A heresy was merely an attempt at such formulation which the considered judgement of the Church rejected; and even those who deny the doctrine of inspiration must at least allow the early Church an uncommon degree of horse sense. Most of the heresies which it condemned were either blind alleys or forms of incipient lunacy.

It is to the former category that we must assign the Arian heresy which figures so largely in the history of Egypt and the Empire during the fourth century. Its founder, Arius, was an Alexandrian presbyter, its chief opponent, St. Athanasius, a native of the city and for many years its Bishop. It must be allowed that Athanasius is not the most attractive of the early Fathers. He was self-willed, authoritarian, ambitious, and intolerant of opposition. I do not believe, with Seeck, that he forged documents, or even that he ever deliberately lied, but to the arts of *suppressio veri* and *suggestio falsi* he was certainly no stranger, and he was a master of billingsgate. Nevertheless, quite apart from the fact that his faults were balanced by very considerable merits and that he mellowed and grew more tolerant with advancing years, an impartial historian cannot but recognize that, on his own premisses, he was right.

The days were past when monotheism was a living issue between Christian and pagan. Whatever the vulgar herd might think, educated pagans were in effect monotheists, who talked almost as often of 'God' as of 'the gods'. The gods were now not so much independent beings as hypostases or particular manifestations of one divine Power.[6] The real issue was the relation between God and man. As the idea of God's transcendence became more deeply impressed on the instructed consciousness, while at the same time the sense of man's sinfulness and degradation increased, it became ever more difficult to find any point of contact between worshipper and worshipped. A whole hierarchy of spirits was imagined by which communication could be effected, but there still remained an unbridged gulf. The great advantage—I had almost said the trump card—of Christianity was its belief in the Incarnation, in a Saviour who was at once God and man, 'God, of the substance of the Father' and 'Man, of the substance of his Mother', as we are informed by the Athanasian Creed (which, by the way, Athanasius did *not* write). In denying the consubstantiality of the Son with the Father Arius broke down the bridge which Christianity had built between a transcendent Deity and the insignificance of man. Hence, when Imperial rescripts thundered against recalcitrant bishops, when Church Councils gathered from the ends of the Empire, when ecclesiastical dignitaries excommunicated one another and mobs of hooligans sacked churches and broke the heads of the opposing faction, the question at stake, whether Christ was *homoousios* or *homoiousios*, little as many of the participants in the struggle could appreciate the theological subtleties involved, was far from being, as it has been called, a mere squabble over a letter, and that the smallest in the Greek alphabet. Whatever ambition, personal or for the see of Alexandria, may have influenced Athanasius (and who shall disentangle the complicated motions of the human mind?), he was fighting, and knew that he was fighting, for a principle vital to the Christian faith. He had much to endure, largely owing to his own intransigence,[7] and three times was driven into exile, but he lived to see his cause triumph. He had opponents, both Arians and the Melitian schismatics, in Egypt itself, but he could count on unswerving support from the bulk of the Egyptian Church.

The character of that Church had now been greatly changed by a new factor. The origins of monasticism, Egypt's chief contribution to Christian development, are obscure. It is hazardous to connect it with the interesting institution of *enkatochê* or *katochê* found in the Sarapis cult, by which recluses in some mysterious way, probably as a result of a divine revelation through a dream, were held to the service of the god and to residence within the great Serapeum at Memphis or elsewhere,[8] but there may have been some enduring tendency in the character of the Egyptians which predisposed them to a withdrawal from the world.[9] Dr. C. B. Welles has recently called attention to the possibility that a pagan community recorded in an inscription from Panopolis may furnish a certain parallel to the later Christian monasticism.[10] There had, of course, always been an ascetic element in Christianity, and from quite early in its history the Egyptian Church had shown encratite tendencies. It is perhaps significant that the first anchorite of whom we hear, St. Paul of Thebes, was a native of Upper Egypt. We may with some probability trace among the causes of the anchoretic movement the emergence of a typically Egyptian mentality. As I have said, the Thebaid was the chief stronghold of Egyptian nationalism and of the priestly cults which were its characteristic expression. Remote from the Hellenized Mediterranean world and living in their narrow valley between the rocky ramparts which fenced off the endless leagues of desert, its inhabitants retained, longer than others, ancient memories and secret fears and superstitions forgotten elsewhere. Modern Protestants and sceptics are too apt to regard monasticism as a cowardly flight from the world and its responsibilities. It may, often enough, have been no more than that in later times, and Paul of Thebes, like others, first sought the desert as a refuge from the persecution of Decius; but the early anchorites would have been horrified at the suggestion that they were running away; on the contrary they were meeting the Adversary on his own ground. From time immemorial the desert had been regarded as the home of evil spirits, the realm of the god Seth, the enemy of Osiris.[11] When an anchorite made his home there he was venturing into the very fortress of the enemy, to fight, all alone save for divine assistance, the battle against the legions of Hell. There, in those appalling solitudes, where by day the fierce sun scorches the rocks and dances in dazzling light on the sand, and by night the stars send down their icy radiance from a clear sky into the vast darkness of the desert, the hermits wrestled with all the powers of evil. A modern psychologist will recognize in their battle an internal struggle, against the lusts of the flesh and the subtler temptations of the mind, but to them and their admirers their adversaries were visible and tangible fiends of Hell. We must remember that they were not endeavouring, in a selfish isolation, merely to save their own souls; they prayed actively for others; they were, we might say, the shock troops of the Church Militant, whose prayers were an effective weapon in the long struggle against the Powers of Darkness. We have ample evidence of the extent to which those in need of spiritual or physical healing appealed to these anchorites. For example, there is in the British Museum an interesting group of papyrus letters addressed to a certain Paphnutius, an anchorite of the fourth century, in which people of various classes ask for his prayers.[12] 'I always know that by your holy prayers I shall be saved from every temptation of the Devil and from every contrivance of men, and now I beg you to remember me in your holy prayers; for after God you are my salvation', writes a certain Ammonius.[13] 'I beg and entreat you, most valued father, to ask for me [help?] from Christ and that I may obtain healing; thus I trust by your prayers to obtain healing, for by ascetics and devotees revelations are manifested. For I am afflicted with a great disease in the shape of a grievous shortness of breath. For thus I have trusted and yet trust that if you pray on my behalf I shall obtain healing'—such is the request of a woman called Valeria;[14] and another petitioner for intercessory prayer in sickness says, 'Now of a truth it is affliction in which I am, where neither from a brother nor from any other can effectual help come save the hope which I expect by our Lord Christ through your prayers.'[15] Finally, in a well-expressed letter from an Athanasius who may conceivably, but improbably, be the great Bishop of Alexandria himself, we find the words, 'for the prayers which you offer are taken on high owing to your holy love, and according as you ask in your holy prayers so will our state prosper'.[16]

The courage and austerities of the anchorites won general admiration; thousands followed their example, and men came from afar, from Italy and Spain and Gaul, to see and talk with these athletes of Christ. Round St. Anthony, the most famous of the hermits, a little community grew up, and before the middle of the fourth century Pachômius established his rule and thus became, in effect, the father of cenobitical monasticism. This is the form most familiar in the West, though there too hermits were common enough, but in Eastern Christianity the solitary life long retained a highly important place side by side with organized communities.

The incredible austerities practised by many of these hermits, like St. Simeon Stylites, may extort a tribute of admiration even from those who have no sympathy with their ideals, and one has only to glance through the *Apophthegmata Patrum* or Sayings of the Fathers to recognize the spiritual insight and moral wisdom attained by some of them; but a humanist will probably regard the development of monasticism in the fourth century as at best a very mixed blessing. For one thing, it meant the withdrawal from active life of thousands of people, and those often men of exceptional vigour and strength of will, at the very time when the safety of the Empire was seriously threatened by shortage of manpower. It meant, too, a great narrowing of the field of men's interest, a terrible impoverishment of cultural life. As we study the record of Byzantine Egypt we can trace clearly this progressive limitation of view, this closing of the mind, this hardening of the mental arteries. Even in the career of Athanasius we find ominous signs of the danger inherent in the support to be derived from droves of ignorant and fanatical monks;

later this danger was only too clearly revealed. It was the monks whom the Patriarch Cyril incited to attack the Jews of Alexandria and expel them from the city; they who, a few years later, in A.D. 415, murdered the noble woman philosopher Hypatia; and their activities are writ large in many later events.

Clement and Origen had succeeded in wedding Greek thought to Christian experience, and the former had shown that a sincere Christian might have a wide and loving appreciation of Greek literature, but Egyptian monasticism was in general hostile to Hellenism and all that it represented. Christianity in fact (not in Egypt only) released hidden nationalist impulses and gave new life to the native idiom. The city-state, which was the most characteristic manifestation of Hellenic life and to which its brilliance and intensity were chiefly due, was also its chief weakness in the process of permeating the Eastern world. Wherever the Greeks went they settled in city communities. These formed little centres of Hellenic culture, but since the Greeks stayed mainly within the city boundaries the influence of this culture on the surrounding country was at best limited. In Egypt, it is true, there were hardly any Greek cities, but even there, with the partial exception of the Fayyûm, the Greeks seem to have been concentrated chiefly in the nome-capitals, leaving the villages in the main to the Egyptians. As we study the Greek papyri of the Ptolemaic and Roman periods, with their many-sided interest, we are rather tempted to think of Egypt as a Greek-speaking country and to ignore the native culture, revealed to us though it is by Demotic legal documents, occasional Demotic tax-receipts or dockets on Greek ones, and some fragments of a Demotic popular literature. But all the time, underground as it

were and little regarded, the native Egyptian life continued, secretly hostile to Hellenism and cherishing its
national pride. Christianity, when it reached this class,
acted as a liberating force, and it was helped by a
change of script. The difficult Demotic writing was
probably known to few outside the priestly caste, but in
the third century the practice began of using the Greek
alphabet, with the addition of six characters taken from
Demotic, for Egyptian texts. It was very possibly for
magical purposes, where exactness in rendering the
magical formulae was essential, that the Greek alphabet,
with its vowel system, was first substituted for Demotic,
which did not write the vowels, but in any case the
possibilities of the innovation were at once perceived by
Christians. First in marginal or interlinear glosses, then
in connected texts, the Scriptures began to be translated
into Coptic, as the new script and the last phase of the
Egyptian language are called; and before the fourth
century was far advanced the whole Bible was available
to Egyptian readers. Far more could read the Greek
script than the Demotic; and moreover Coptic writers
used a more modern and colloquial form of Egyptian
than the Demotic scribes. Thus an abundant Coptic
literature, Biblical, theological, and liturgical but very
rarely secular, grew up; and for the first time since the
third century B.C. the very soul of Egypt found un-
fettered expression. Many of the monks and anchorites
were of Egyptian race; indeed, as I have suggested,
monasticism was probably in some degree a native
Egyptian product. The Egyptian Church thus acquired
a strongly nationalist character. The Egyptians, without an admixture of Greek blood, have never shown
much capacity for abstract philosophical thought; the
mystical significance given to many Egyptian legends,

like those of Isis and Osiris, was due to Greek religious thinkers. The monks who flocked at the tail of their Patriarch to the Councils of the Church had certainly little comprehension of the theological subtleties involved; what they could understand was the political opposition of Egypt to the Imperial government. Hence it was natural that when Constantinople, the new capital, was heretical, as under the Arian Emperor Constantius, Egypt should be Catholic, when Constantinople was Catholic, Egypt should be heretical.

The schism which cut off the bulk of the Egyptian Church from Catholic Christendom occurred in the fifth century. Ostensibly the point at issue was one of doctrine. Theological thought was still occupied with the attempt to define the mystery of the Incarnation: if Christ was both God and Man, had he two natures? And if so, what was their exact relationship? Arius had denied the consubstantiality of the Son with the Father, though he had not questioned Christ's divinity in a certain sense. The opposite error was to ignore or minimize the humanity. In its extreme form the monophysite heresy, though it allowed the existence of two natures before their union in the Incarnation, held that there was but one afterwards. Thus the human nature was extinguished by the divine, it was not subsumed into it, and once more the bridge between God and man was broken. That is a simplified and perhaps a not wholly accurate statement, but the point was really one of extreme subtlety and by no means easy to grasp. The Catholic leaders made repeated attempts to arrive at a compromise, until at length the dividing line was very tenuous, but in vain. The dispute was complicated by personal animosities and by the rivalry between the three great sees, Rome, Constantinople, and Alexandria;

as the late Jean Maspero said with justice, 'in the main monophysitism is not a heresy, it is merely a schismatic intention'.

The occupant of the see of Alexandria from 412 to 444 was St. Cyril, whose views, though they emphasized specially the divinity of Christ, remained within the limits of orthodoxy. While deficient in the very considerable virtues of his great predecessor, Athanasius, he showed in an exaggerated form the same faults as he. He was overbearing, turbulent, greedy of power, and utterly unscrupulous in the means he employed. It was Cyril who incited the monks and the rabble to expel the Jews from Alexandria; he did his utmost to suppress the philosophical school in the university, with its pagan associations, and, if not the instigator, was at least the passive approver of the disturbances which led to the murder of Hypatia. At the Council of Ephesus in 431 he was mainly responsible for the condemnation and banishment of Nestôrius, the Patriarch of Constantinople, and by lavish bribery he succeeded in escaping responsibility for the grave irregularities which marred the council. His successor, Dioscorus, had all his faults but lacked his political *flair* and finesse, and he committed himself to a monophysite position. At the so-called 'Robber' Council of Ephesus in 449 he triumphed, but by methods so outrageous that a strong combination was formed against him, and at the Council of Chalcedon in 451, which issued the famous statement declaring that Christ is 'consubstantial with his Father as regards his Godhead, and consubstantial with us as regards his Manhood', and that he was 'made known to us in two natures', Dioscorus was condemned and deposed. Prôterius, appointed to succeed him, was torn to pieces by a mob set on him by a monophysite rival,

Timothy Ailouros, 'Timothy the Cat', as he was nick-
named. Henceforward the mass of Egyptian Christianity was in schism from the Catholic Church.

Schism, though sometimes necessary, is always an
evil, for by emphasizing points of difference it tends to
narrowness even in the parent body and to provinciality
of thought in the schismatic one. So it proved here.
The Catholic or Melkite party, as it was called, dependent on the support of the Imperial government and
therefore obnoxious to the majority of the people,
enjoyed but little prestige and commanded a scanty
following. The Monophysites or Jacobites, supported
by the ignorant monks, who were hostile to Hellenic
culture in all its forms, were quite incapable of making
any important contribution to the thought of the age.
Thus Egypt, whose capital, Alexandria, had been in the
second and third centuries the seat of the famous Catechetical School and even in the fourth had produced in
Athanasius a major figure of ecclesiastical history,
became a provincial backwater.

Cyril had not succeeded in suppressing the philosophical school of Alexandria, and as late as the second
half of the fifth century the university contained a circle
of pagan philosophers, into whose life a petition preserved in a papyrus gives us an attractive glimpse.[17]
These men, however, though their culture was doubtless
strongly tinged by Hellenism, were ardent nationalists;
one of them is the reputed author of an extant treatise
on the hieroglyphic script. Even in Alexandria Hellenism was threatened; in the rest of Egypt the adverse
influences of monasticism and the nationalist reaction
were reinforced by the economic decline, which the
reforms of Diocletian had been powerless to arrest.

A leading feature of those reforms had been the sim-

plification of the tax system, but the advantages which
this promised were illusory. In fixing the units of pro-
duction regard was had, it is true, to differences of
quality, and fractions were no doubt admitted, but
even so the method of assessment was too rough and
ready for safety in a time of economic stringency. For
example, in Syria (we have no figures for Egypt) the
iugum for olive-yards was 225 trees. Thus, supposing a
man owned 240 trees he would be assessed for one
iugum and a fraction. If, therefore, some of his trees
were old and not very productive it might pay him to
cut down fifteen of them and thereby reduce his liability
to a single *iugum*. Similarly the owner of arable land
might find it advantageous to leave the less fertile
portions uncultivated. That this actually happened is
known, with the consequence that in many places, in
Africa and Syria no less than in Egypt, land began to
go out of cultivation. We can trace the process with
special clearness in the Fayyûm, where villages, popu-
lous and flourishing in the second century and even in
the third considerable centres of population, had in the
early years of the fourth been abandoned by most of
their inhabitants, and by the end of the century had
been reduced, as they remained till modern times, to
great mounds of sand covering the ruins of deserted
dwellings. The revenue from a province in which this
process was going on tended to shrink, but the government's expenses showed no such diminution. The
northern frontiers, constantly invaded by the Teutonic
barbarians, called for a large military force, and the
Persians were always a threat in the East. Furthermore, the Diocletianic system needed an elaborate
bureaucracy. To prevent peculation and oppression
a network of checks and counter-checks was devised,

one official set to supervise another. All these officials had to be paid, and in addition to their pay they all wanted their perquisites, their *sportula*. So much a matter of course were these *sportula* that they came to be actually allowed for in the taxes, much as many modern hotels and restaurants endeavour to replace tipping by a charge of 10 per cent. for 'service'. The government could not, if it would, reduce its demands; and the municipal senates and their organs, responsible for the delivery of the full communal quota, were forced to apply the screw to the peasantry. If they still failed to raise the amount required their own property was drawn on to supply the deficit. Thus economic stress was a two-way traffic, and peasantry and senatorial class found themselves faced with a common ruin. The government, honestly anxious to prevent this, might issue regulations and appeals against exploitation, but nothing short of a reduction in the quota could supply the remedy. Unable to consider that, the authorities as usual had resort to compulsion. When so much depended on the productivity of the land, its cultivator, whether tenant or owner, must be prevented from leaving it, must be tied to the soil he tilled. The senatorial class, in the last resort responsible for the quota, must no less be maintained at strength;[18] the son of a senator must succeed to his father's liability, and equally the son of the shipper, charged with the transport of corn and money taxes to Constantinople, must himself become a shipper, the son of a donkey-driver become a donkey-driver. Thus, by an inexorable logic, came into being the Byzantine servile state, a vast hierarchy of caste and calling, each hereditary and inescapable.[19] The rigidity was not, indeed, absolute. We hear of people rising from humble origins to the highest eminence, chiefly by one of the three avenues, the army, the civil service, or the Church, but these were men of exceptional talents or initiative; the average man was fixed for life in the station to which he was born.

In the Ptolemaic period, if a peasant found his position intolerable, he could take sanctuary at the altar of the King or in one of the numerous temples which enjoyed the right of asylum, only to leave it if his grievances were remedied. Under Roman rule this right had been greatly restricted, and the obvious resource was to flee to the swamps or the desert and join some robber band. There was, however, one other possibility. As I said in the previous chapter, there were men even in the third century who made a profit amid the general decline. Initiative and energy, backed by capital, can turn other men's misfortunes to their own advantage. Already at that time great private estates were in process of formation. Their owners, balancing the profits of one farm against the loss on another, could bear without serious embarrassment the demands of the tax officials; and we may be sure that in a venal age the man with money had means of procuring preferential treatment. Already before the end of the fourth century the wealthier owners, the *potentiores*, had secured from the government (probably because the latter found it difficult otherwise to collect the required quota) the right, known as *autopragia*, to collect the taxes due from their own estates and pay them direct, not through the local collectors, to the provincial treasury. The small owner, then, threatened with ruin, could turn for protection to some powerful neighbour, could surrender to him his own land, which he held henceforth as a lessee, doing service to his landlord in exchange for the assumption by the latter of the ultimate responsibility for payment of the taxes. From being an owner he had become a tenant, tied to his land, which now belonged to another, had become a *colonus adscripticius*, in fact a serf.

The Imperial authorities did not relish the development of the patronate, and one constitution after another forbade it, but in vain. Prohibitions are fruitless against the irresistible pressure of economic conditions. At last, in 415, the government capitulated. A constitution of that year provided that all who before 397 held land under the title of patron should be left in possession of it, assuming liability for all the obligations incumbent on their *coloni*, but that the name of patron should cease. This concession gave to the position of the *coloni adscripticii* a legal status, but it did not, as was intended, prevent the further development of the patronate, though owing to the curious scarcity of papyri dating from the fifth century we are not able to trace the process in any detail.

When we reach the sixth century, which is well documented, we are struck by the change which has taken place. The first novelty which we perceive is an administrative one. The *pagi* into which the nome had been divided, each under a *praepositus*, have disappeared. The whole rural area now forms a single district, financially administered by an official called a pagarch. This change certainly occurred in the fifth century, probably during the reign of the Emperor Leo I (457–74).[20] The control of the pagarch did not, in normal circumstances, cover the whole territory, for the estates of the great landowners possessing the right of *autopragia* paid their taxes not through him but direct to the provincial treasurer; and the same privilege had been granted to several monasteries and churches and (no doubt as a make-weight to the power of the nobility) to some of the more important villages. The pagarch was an Imperial official, appointed by and responsible to the Emperor. He had no authority over the municipality, which after the creation of his office ceased to be responsible for the finances of the rural territory.

Another momentous change in administration occurred in 554,[21] when Justinian issued his thirteenth edict. This has come down to us in a mutilated form, but it is possible to reconstruct the main provisions of what is lost from the portion which remains. There had already been several readjustments of the provinces established by Diocletian, and in 382 they had ceased to form part of the diocese of the Orient and had become a separate diocese, the Prefect of Egypt, with the title of Augustal, having ultimate authority over the whole country; but hitherto the Diocletianic principle of a division between military and civil authority had been maintained. It was now abandoned. By the new arrangement the unity of Egypt was for the first time dissolved; the Augustal Prefect of Egypt ceased to have any control over the other provinces, which were all alike placed under the immediate authority of the Prefect of the Praetorium of the Orient, and each governor received both military and civil powers. Henceforth Egypt (apart from Libya) fell into four co-ordinate provinces: Aegyptus, under a Duke with the title of Augustal; Augustamnica, under a Duke; Arcadia, under a Count; and the Thebaid, under an Augustal Duke. The last-named and the first two were each divided into two sub-provinces, governed by purely civil *praesides*.

Economically, the chief novelty we notice in the sixth century is the great estates of the noble families. Concerning one of these families we are well informed, owing to the fact that many of its papers are preserved among the papyri found at Oxyrhynchus.[22] The first member of it who can be certainly identified is Flavius Apiôn, a man of consular rank; it was customary at this period to confer this honorary dignity on prominent men who had not actually filled the office of consul. He was apparently alive in 497, when his son, Flavius Stratêgius, is addressed by the court title of *comes domesticorum*, or Count of the Household Troops.[23] Stratêgius himself later obtained the consular dignity and the patriciate and held the high Imperial office of Count of the Sacred Largesses.[24] His son, Flavius Apiôn II, was actually *consul ordinarius* in 539, was a Patrician, and from 548 to 550 was Duke of the Thebaid. His son was Flavius Stratêgius II, succeeded before 590 by a third Apiôn. The last member of the family of whom we hear is a third Stratêgius, probably the son of this Apiôn. After 625 the family disappears, perhaps merely because none of its later papers have survived.

A family of Middle Egypt which through successive generations enjoyed the consular and patrician dignities and not only filled the highest administrative posts in the country itself but actually contributed a consul to the Empire was obviously an important one, and the papyri show that the Apiôn family did in fact possess immense wealth and power. It owned estates not only in the Oxyrhynchite but in at least two other nomes as well, the Cynopolite nome and the Fayyûm or Arsinoite nome. In the Oxyrhynchite nome many entire villages belonged to it. Like other great families of which we hear, it had its private army of hired soldiers, the so-called *buccellarii*, who, as we know from the estate accounts, included men of Germanic race. Like other families, again, it had its private prisons (a practice forbidden, but in vain, by Imperial constitutions), its own postal service with regular posting stations, its racing-stable, its public baths and hospitals, its banks and counting-houses, its host of officials, secretaries, accountants, tax-collectors, and the like; it possessed its fleet of Nile boats, and even paid its taxes not to the provincial treasurer but direct to Alexandria; it founded and endowed, and no doubt controlled, churches and monasteries.

A study of these great families inevitably suggests a comparison with the feudal lordships of western Europe. The analogy is not, indeed, complete. The feudal system of the West was essentially military, the free tenant holding his land on condition of rendering service in war to his feudal lord, whether direct to the king, like the tenants-in-chief, or to a mesne lord. The tenure in Egypt was not military, and the estates were not compact blocks of territory as in France and to some, though a lesser, extent in England and Wales, but were scattered about the country; sometimes part of the territory of a village belonged to such an estate while part was held by small owners owing it no service.[25] In the West the feudal lord lived in his castle, in the midst of his lands; in Egypt the great landlord had his house— a palace it must have been in the case of the Apiôn family—in the town, Oxyrhynchus or Hermopolis or even Alexandria. Yet the position of these landlords was sufficiently like that of a feudal baron to justify us in calling them semi-feudal; and it is interesting to compare the two systems in their likeness and their difference. In the West the feudal lordship was a replica in little of the kingdom to which it belonged: just as the king had his tenants-in-chief owing him fealty and service, so each feudal lord had his own vassals, similarly bound to him. The Egyptian estate, on the other hand, reproduced in little the bureaucratic empire of which it formed a part; its organization and its hierarchy of officials were modelled on the Imperial bureaucracy. Indeed it is sometimes impossible, in dealing with a papyrus document of this period, to be certain whether the persons whose titles are mentioned in it were Imperial officials or the servants of some great family.

Over against these powerful lords, with their little courts and the splendour of their establishments, was the mass of the rural population. It fell into two broad classes, on the one hand the *coloni* of the great estates, serfs bound to the soil and the service of their landlords, on the other hand the free cultivators owning their own land or renting land from the lesser proprietors. Though nominally free, these too were bound to the soil, forbidden in the interests of the State to leave their holdings; and since the pagarchs to whom, except in the case of autopract villages, they paid their taxes, were drawn from the ranks of the nobility (the Apiôn family, for example, held the office of pagarch for long periods), their position cannot have differed greatly from that of the serfs on the great estates. Indeed, as it was to the interest of a landlord to see that his *coloni* were reasonably prosperous, whereas no such consideration applied to free peasants, and the landlords were wealthy and seem sometimes to have been model landlords, it may well have been worse. This presumption is borne out by the evidence of the papyri. Autopract villages were perhaps somewhat better off, but their position was not a happy one. The pagarchs, alike as landlords with the right of *autopragia* and in their official capacity, resented the grant of the privilege to villages. The privilege of *autopragia* became inoperative if tax payments fell into arrear, and it seems in any case not to have applied to certain local taxes. If, therefore, a pagarch did find occasion to intervene in the affairs of an autopract village his hand was apt to be heavy, as we know from the papyri discovered on the site of the village of Aphrodite in the Thebaid. A raid by disorderly soldiers, houses sacked and burned, water diverted, fields laid waste, nuns raped, leading proprietors imprisoned and tortured—such were the results of a quarrel with the pagarch, and this in a village which as a precaution and to reinforce its autopract status had placed itself under the Imperial protection.[26] But, as Justinian remarks in a rescript relating to a case of oppression by a pagarch, 'the intrigues of Theodosius proved stronger than our commands'.[27] The semi-feudal nobility were at hand, with all their *buccellarii*; the Emperor, however benevolent his intentions, was far away, in Constantinople.

How great a gulf had opened between wealthy noble and *colonus* may best be judged by looking at petitions and comparing them with similar documents of an earlier period. Here, for example, is the beginning of one written about the year 243 B.C.: 'To King Ptolemy, greeting, Antigonus. I am being unjustly treated by Patrôn, the superintendent of police in the lower toparchy.'[28] It is a minor official in a village of Middle Egypt petitioning the all-powerful Ptolemy III Euergetês; yet he addresses the king without servility or verbiage, as man to man. Now compare a petition addressed in the sixth century by a *colonus* of the Apiôn estate to his landlord: 'To my good master, lover of Christ, lover of the poor, all-esteemed and most magnificent Patrician and Duke of the Thebaid, Apiôn, from Anoup, your miserable slave upon your estate called Phacra.'[29] Even more striking are the opening sentences of a petition addressed to a duke by the autopract village of Aphrodite in 567:[30]

'To Flavius Triadius Marianus Michael Gabriel Constantine Theodore Martyrius Julianus Athanasius, the most renowned general and consular and most magnificent Patrician of the Prefect Justin, Duke and Augustal of the Thebaid for the second year. Petition and supplication from your most pitiable slaves, the wretched small owners and inhabitants of the all-miserable village of Aphrodite, which is under the sacred household and your magnificent authority. All justice and just dealing for ever illuminate the proceedings of your pre-eminently excellent and magnificent authority, which we have long expected as the dead in Hades once awaited the coming of the Christ, the everlasting God. For after him, our master God, the Saviour, the Helper, the true and merciful Benefactor, we set all our hopes of salvation upon your Highness, who are among all men praised and bruited abroad . . . whence without fear we are come to grovel in the track of your immaculate footsteps and inform you of the state of our affairs.'

In such a world what place could there be for Hellenism, the civilization of free men, with free minds? Its chief centres, outside the Greek cities, Alexandria and Ptolemais, had been the nome-capitals. We are much less well informed about municipal affairs in the sixth century than at an earlier date, but the fact is probably in itself significant. These old nome-capitals, which in the second century had prided themselves on their Hellenic traditions and enjoyed the ephebic festivals, which even in the difficult days of the third century had assumed pompous titles, like 'the illustrious and most illustrious city of the Oxyrhynchites' or 'the great, ancient, most august, and most illustrious city of Hermes', and in the fourth had attained full municipal status, were becoming less and less important and enjoying less and less liberty. Their rural areas, so far as they did not possess *autopragia*, were under an Imperial official, the pagarch. The pagarch himself and the great family from which he sprang lived in the city and must have been in a position to influence the decisions of the senate at every turn. In one papyrus of about the end of the sixth century we find the *defensor* of Cynopolis saying that he has expressed the gratitude he feels towards his correspondent 'to our common master, the most renowned *illustris*, the landlord's agent'[31] (the landlord is probably the head of the Apiôn family), and in another, dated in 587, a deputy *defensor* appears as a tenant on the Apiôn estates.[32] The office of *defensor* had been created, as I have said, to protect the poor against the rich; yet we now see its holders become the subservient vassals of the great nobles. As for the intellectual temper of the time it is sufficient to remark that the monks were intolerant of Hellenism, that the bulk of the Egyptian Church was monophysite,[33] and that to be monophysite was, almost automatically, to take the nationalist attitude of hostility to the wider culture of the Imperial capital.

Hellenism was manifestly dying in the sixth century, but its death was a long and slow process. Discoveries at Antinoopolis and elsewhere show that Greek and even Latin literature was still being read and that sixth-century readers still had access to much which is now lost. It is particularly striking that so difficult a Roman poet as Juvenal was at this time being studied, with an elaborate commentary, in the Thebaid.[34] The papyri from the village of Aphrodite have brought us acquainted with a native of that place who attained some success as a lawyer and notary, was an assiduous writer of Greek verse (in which he achieved the dis-

tinction, for what it is worth, of being the worst Greek
poet whose works have come down to us), read Homer,
the Anacreontic poems, and Nonnus, compiled a
Greek-Coptic glossary which reveals a knowledge,
perhaps acquired at second hand, of somewhat out-of-
the-way classical literature, and owned not only a
manuscript of Menander's plays but, what is more surprising, of the *Demes* of Eupolis, a poet of that Old
Comedy which some modern scholars had supposed to
be virtually unknown to the general reader at this
period.[35] If such studies were pursued by a village
notable in the Thebaid, how much more likely is it that
Hellenic culture was still active in the more important
centres!

Nevertheless Hellenism was clearly doomed in Egypt,
and when we reach the seventh century we find clear
evidence that the Greek language, with all which it
implied, was rapidly losing ground in the country.
Coptic was increasingly used for legal and other documents, and even Church dignitaries might be ignorant
of Greek, like Abraham, Bishop of Hermônthis, whose
will, contained in a British Museum papyrus, informs us
that it was dictated in Coptic, to be written for him in
Greek.[36] Literary papyri surviving from this period are
few in number and drawn from a narrower range of
authors; and seventh-century Greek papyri containing
such Christian texts as hymns, liturgical prayers, and
portions of Scripture (often used as amulets) are frequently so extraordinarily corrupt as to show that the
scribes had only the haziest understanding of what they
were writing.[37]

In the year 608 Hêraclius, the governor of Africa,
revolted against Phôcas, the brutal usurper who had
dethroned and murdered the Emperor Maurice. Hêra-

clius was himself too old to welcome the burden of Imperial rule; it was his son, Hêraclius the younger, who was destined for the purple. A plan was formed by which Nicêtas, son of the governor's second-in-command, should attempt the conquest of Egypt, while the younger Hêraclius made for Thessalonica. Nicêtas advanced along the north coast and after some hard fighting had secured command of Egypt by the end of 609. Meantime Hêraclius had occupied Thessalonica and in 610 sailed for Constantinople. His fleet appeared before the city on the 3rd October. The tyranny of Phôcas had alienated the bulk of the people, and two days later he was handed over to Hêraclius and put to death. Hêraclius now became Emperor. He was a general of outstanding capacity, a man conscientiously resolved to do what he could for the safety of the Empire, and capable of vigour and determination, though apparently subject, probably from physical reasons, to recurrent fits of inertia and depression. He had reasons enough for discouragement. For some years past the Imperial armies had suffered a series of defeats. The Persian king, Chosroës, was invading the Empire from the east; the Slavonic Avars were ever threatening in the north. The fidelity of Priscus, the commander-in-chief of the army, was doubtful. The treasury was half empty, and there was a serious shortage of man-power. Moreover, it would seem that there was felt everywhere a sense of impending doom, a loss of nerve and self-confidence.

At first matters went from bad to worse, despite strenuous efforts on the part of Hêraclius. Deeper and deeper did Chosroës penetrate into the Empire. In 614 came a crowning disaster, the fall of Jerusalem. In 616 the Persians invaded and conquered Egypt. The whole of Asia Minor, too, was now in their hands, and their armies could look across the narrow waters of the Bosphorus into the heart of the Imperial city, resplendent on its hills. It seemed the hour of doom; and had the Persian power at sea equalled that on land East Rome might have fallen eight centuries too soon and left Europe without its eastern bastion. Fortunately the naval assault was beaten off, and no further attempt was made. In 622 Hêraclius, after solemnly committing Constantinople to the protection of God and the Mother of God, crossed into Asia Minor and in a brilliant campaign liberated the whole of it; in 623 he set out to invade Persia itself and won resounding successes. Then, in 626, a fresh danger appeared; the Avar hordes flooded down from the north and beleaguered Constantinople by land and sea. Again disaster threatened; panic reigned in the streets, and it seemed that only divine intervention could save the city. From all the churches prayers went up to the Mother of God to come to the help of her people, and it was remarked as a token of her power that when the churches of SS. Cosmas and Damian and of St. Nicholas were burned her shrine at Blachernae escaped unharmed. The prayers were answered; the boats of the Avars were repulsed and sunk, and their army retreated northwards. On the 3rd April 628 a Persian embassy brought Hêraclius the news of the death of Chosroës and the succession of his son, and with it an offer of peace. The terms required the complete withdrawal of the Persian forces from the Empire; and accordingly Egypt too was evacuated and was once again brought under Byzantine rule.

Not, however, for long. In 622 had occurred an event fraught with momentous consequences alike for Byzantium and for Persia. In that year Mahomet, discouraged by the reception of his teaching among his fellow-townsmen, fled from Mecca to Medina and thereby, though neither he nor his followers realized it, inaugurated a new chronological epoch, the era of the Hegira. When he died, on the 7th June 632, the larger part of Arabia had already accepted Islam.

Meanwhile Hêraclius, anxious to consolidate the Empire, had made great efforts to win back the Copts to the Catholic Church. He compromised so far as to accept the monothelite heresy, which held that Christ had indeed two natures, contrary to the monophysite doctrine, but only one will. It seemed to him that dyophysites and monophysites might here find a meeting-place. But the Egyptians were not prepared to compromise; what they wanted was to oppose Constantinople. In 631 Hêraclius appointed a bishop named Cyrus who had embraced the monothelite doctrine to be Patriarch of Alexandria and at the same time Augustal Prefect of Egypt. It was an unfortunate choice. Cyrus, whom our scanty evidence leaves a baffling and rather shadowy figure, seems to have been a man of an impatient temper, and when he found that the Copts were not to be won over to the new doctrine he embarked on a savage campaign of persecution, thus alienating the very people whom he had been sent to conciliate.

There was need of whatever loyalty could be won. After Mahomet's death the first Caliph Abû Bakr was faced by a revolt of some of the tribes. This was successfully crushed; before long the whole of Arabia was subject to the Caliph's authority, and its hardy and warlike tribes, grown too numerous for the scanty resources of their country and flushed with all the ardour of a new and militant faith, were ripe for expansion. Soon their armies were carrying all before them in Syria. In 637 came the first clash between them and the Persians, and before their attack the great empire of the Sassanids went down in utter and final ruin.

In 639 one of the leading Arab generals, 'Amr ibn al-'Āṣ, who had played a great part in the conquest of Syria, won from Omar, the second Caliph, a reluctant consent for the invasion of Egypt, though only four thousand men could be spared for the attempt, and the Arabs had no artillery for the siege of fortresses. According to Arab historians, 'Amr had arrived near the site of the Battle of Raphia when a messenger overtook him with a letter from the Caliph. Suspecting what its contents might be, he did not open it till he reached al-'Arîsh. Then he broke the seal and read the contents: 'From the Commander of the Faithful to 'Amr b. al-'Āṣ. If this letter reaches you before you have crossed the frontier of Egypt, return; but if it arrives after you have entered Egypt, proceed, and God be with you.' He turned to his staff: 'Is this place in Syria or in Egypt?' he asked. 'In Egypt', was the answer. 'Amr then read the letter aloud and announced: 'The army will advance, and God be with us.'

What followed was not quite the miracle that some have taken it to be. 'Amr had but four thousand men when he crossed the frontier, but before the decisive battle of Hêliopolis he was joined by reinforcements amounting to some twelve thousand more. The numbers of the Imperial troops have been greatly exaggerated; they probably amounted to no more than about thirty thousand in all, scattered about the country in various garrisons and many of them probably not of high quality.[38] It was impossible, moreover, to concentrate them readily at any one point. The fatal results were now seen of Justinian's policy in breaking the unity of Egypt and giving to all the governors co-ordinate authority. Each thought only of his own sphere; we are even informed that the Duke of the Thebaid, on the approach of the Arabs, hastily collected the taxes and decamped with the proceeds to Alexandria.

After defeating the Imperial army at Hêliopolis 'Amr laid siege to Babylon, the great fortress at the head of the Delta. The Fayyûm was occupied, but Babylon held out, and 'Amr opened negotiations with Cyrus, who agreed to the draft of a treaty of surrender.[39] He went to Constantinople to submit it to the Emperor, who at once repudiated it and sent him into exile. But Hêraclius was now a dying man, and with his death on the 11th February 641 divided councils in the capital delayed the dispatch of reinforcements. Babylon fell in April 641, and the Arabs marched on Alexandria, strongly opposed by the Imperial troops, who showed more spirit than their leaders. Cyrus had by now been reinstated, and finding Alexandria torn by faction, and too readily despairing of success, he concluded with the Arabs a treaty providing for the payment of a tribute by the city, for its evacuation by the Imperial forces within eleven months, and for the protection of Christians and Jews. No help came from Constantinople, and on the 17th September 642 the Imperial army sailed out of the harbour. On the 29th of the same month the Arabs marched into the great city, wondering at its miles of marble colonnades and its splendid palaces.

The story of Hellenistic Egypt was at an end, and the country, whose gaze had been turned by the victories of Alexander from the East and the past to the West and the future, had returned to the Oriental world of which it had formed a part. But the world, whether Eastern or Western, was very different from that which Alexander knew. The oracle of Ammon was silent. The great temples of Egypt were abandoned or turned into Coptic monasteries. In the Christian churches and monasteries of Europe and Asia men debated subtle points of a theology constructed by Greek thought out of the teaching and the life and death of a Jewish prophet, and already from the minaret of many a mosque in Arabia and the neighbouring lands sounded the cry of the Muezzin, *Allâhu akbar; lâ ilâha illa 'llâh*, 'God is great; there is no god but God'. Presently Islam, described by Mommsen as 'the executioner of Hellenism', was itself to borrow largely from Greek science and Greek philosophy, handing them on in its turn to the thinkers of western Europe. Egyptian craftsmen were to be employed on the mosques of Jerusalem and Damascus, and many a decorative motive, acanthus-leaf and vine-tendril, would pass from Graeco-Coptic art into the stock-in-trade of Islamic architects, and later would leave its traces here and there in the Christian buildings of southern Europe. Alexander's work, cut short by his premature death, misunderstood and set aside by his successors, nevertheless lived after him. Europe and Asia had indeed been wedded after a fashion, though not quite in the way he designed, and neither of them could ever be the same again.

NOTES

CHAPTER I

1. Herod. ii. 35. Rawlinson's translation.
2. Herod. ii. 5.
3. Usually called 'Lake Moeris', but Sir Alan H. Gardiner has shown (*Journ. Eg. Arch.* xxix, 1943, pp. 37–46) that Herodotus' phrase, ἡ Μοίριος καλεομένη λίμνη ('the so-called lake of Moeris') is almost certainly correct.
4. The process of making papyrus is described by Pliny, *Hist. Nat.* xiii. 74, 77–82. See N. Lewis, *L'Industrie du Papyrus*, pp. 46 ff., where the relevant passages are quoted, translated, and discussed.
5. In using this expression I follow the old view that the manufacture of papyrus was a state monopoly under the Byzantine Empire. N. Lewis, op. cit., pp. 159–63, argues against this. He may be right, though I do not find his arguments wholly convincing.
6. A very interesting and enlightening description of the make-up of a particularly well preserved codex (of several tablets), containing a Latin will, is given, with facsimiles and diagrams, by O. Guéraud and P. Jouguet, 'Un testament latin *per aes et libram* de 142 après J.-C.', in *Études de Papyrologie*, vi, 1940, pp. 1 ff., plates i–vi.
7. For Thmouis papyri see P. Ryl. ii. 213–22, 426–33 (*a*); V. Martin, 'Un document administratif du nome de Mendès', in *Studien zur Palaeographie und Papyruskunde*, xvii, pp. 9–48, and references there, p. 9. It may be added here that similar accidental causes account for the few cases of the discovery of papyri elsewhere than in Egypt. These are: Herculaneum, where the lava which buried the town preserved a large collection of papyrus rolls in a house which was the local centre of the Epicurean school of philosophy; Dura-Eurôpos, on the Euphrates, where in the middle of the third century A.D. the Roman garrison, in anticipation of a Persian assault, strengthened the wall at one point by piling a mass of earth against it, covering the buildings beneath, and thus preserving against the effects of the climate the vellum and papyrus documents contained in them; and Auja al-Hafîr in

southern Palestine, where a mass of papyrus rolls was similarly preserved by being stored under the floor of a ruined church.

8. Others are in the Library of the University of Michigan, that of Princeton University (the property of Mr. John H. Scheide), at Vienna, and in the collection of Mr. Wilfred Merton.

9. F. Preisigke and E. Kiessling, *Wörterbuch der griechischen Papyrusurkunden mit Einschluss der griechischen Inschriften Aufschriften Ostraka Mumienschilder usw. aus Ägypten*, 1925, vol. i *A–K*, vol. ii *Λ–Ω*, 1927, vol. iii *Besondere Wörterliste*, 1931. [Referred to as **WB.**] Heft 1 of vol. iv has now appeared (1944).

10. F. Preisigke, *Namenbuch enthaltend alle griechischen, lateinischen, ägyptischen, hebräischen, arabischen und sonstigen semitischen und nicht-semitischen Menschennamen, soweit sie in griechischen Urkunden (Papyri, Ostraka, Inschriften, Mumienschildern usw.) Ägyptens sich vorfinden*, 1922. [**Namenbuch.**] A list of place names forms section 16a of the special indices in vol. iii of the *Wörterbuch*.

11. *Sammelbuch Griechischer Urkunden aus Ägypten.* Begun by F. Preisigke, who was responsible for vols. i (nos. 1–6000), 1915, and ii (indices), 1922, and continued after his death in successive volumes by F. Bilabel, whose death during the war has caused its (it is to be hoped temporary) suspension. [**SB.**]

12. *Berichtigungsliste der Griechischen Papyrusurkunden aus Ägypten*: vol. i by F. Preisigke, 1922; vol. ii (which includes ostraca) by F. Bilabel, [1929], 1933. [**BL.**]

13. O. Gradenwitz, *Heidelberger Konträrindex der griechischen Papyrusurkunden*, 1931. A contrary index of personal names is being prepared by a Dutch papyrologist, Dr. E. P. Wegener.

14. *Archiv für Papyrusforschung.* [**Archiv.**] Articles in German, English, French, Italian are admitted to this journal.

15. *Études de Papyrologie.*

16. *Journal of Papyrology.*

17. P. Rev. (see below, list of papyrus publications).

18. P. Tebt. iii. 703.

19. B.G.U. v, *Der Gnomon des Idios Logos*; 1st part, text, by W. Schubart, 1919, 2nd part, commentary, by Woldemar Graf Uxkull-Gyllenband, 1934.

20. See the monograph, *Ptolemais in Oberägypten*, by G. Plaumann, Leipziger Historische Abhandlungen, Heft xviii, 1910.

CHAPTER II

1. A recent discussion of the question is that by P. Jouguet, 'Alexandre à l'oasis d'Ammon et le témoignage de Callisthène', in *Bull. de l'Inst. d'Égypte*, xxvi, 1944, pp. 91–107. On p. 92, note 1, is given a list of previous discussions.

2. W. W. Tarn, 'Alexander the Great and the Unity of Mankind' (*Proc. Brit. Acad.* xix, 1933, pp. 123–66). See Plutarch, *Alex.* 27: 'He is reported to have said that God is the common Father of all men, but that He counts the best men peculiarly His own.'

3. P. Eleph. 1 = M. *Chrest.* 283, Hunt and Edgar, *Select Papyri*, i. 1.

4. V. Tscherikower, *Mizraim*, iv–v, 1937, pp. 43–5, shows that the policy of Ptolemy II in Syria was very different; he enumerates five Greek cities known to have been founded in his reign. But Philadelphus' policy in Egypt was, like that of his successors, the same as his father's.

5. See Kornemann, 'Die Satrapenpolitik des ersten Lagiden', in *Raccolta . . . in onore di Giacomo Lumbroso*, pp. 235–45. I followed this view in my article 'Alexandria', in *Journ. Eg. Arch.* xiii, 1927, p. 172.

6. See M. Rostovtzeff, *The Social and Economic History of the Hellenistic World*, i. 275, where the question is left open. Greeks were certainly subject to some 'liturgies' (compulsory services).

7. P. Col. Zen. 66, a letter from a non-Greek, whom the editors are inclined to regard as an Arab but who may perhaps have been an Egyptian, shows, whatever the nationality of the writer, the sense of racial inferiority from which some Asiatics and Egyptians suffered: 'They look down on me because I am a barbarian. So I beg of you to be good enough to order them to let me have what is owing to me and for the future to pay me regularly, so that I shan't starve to death because I can't speak Greek (?).' (The editors translate *hellenizein* as 'act the Hellene', but even if the Greek letter was written by the man himself, which is by no means certain, the word may merely be an exaggerated way of saying 'I am not at home in Greek'; cf. Préaux, *Grecs en Égypte*, p. 69.[10])

8. P. Lond. i, p. 48, no. 43.

9. Clement of Alexandria (*Protrept.* iv) states that the image was, according to some, sent to Ptolemy II Philadelphus, but there is no doubt that it was Ptolemy I who introduced the cult.

10. UPZ. i, pp. 18–37. For Sarapis see also C. E. Visser, *Götter und Kulte im ptolemäischen Alexandrien*, pp. 20–3.

11. The frequency, however, of cult meals in honour of Sarapis at Oxyrhynchus (and doubtless elsewhere) shows that the cult was by no means confined to Alexandria.

12. An excellent appreciation of Egyptian influences on the Hellenistic culture of Egypt is given by Mlle Claire Préaux in her 'Les Égyptiens dans la civilisation hellénistique d'Égypte', in *Chronique d'Égypte*, xvii. 35 (1943), pp. 148–60. She emphasizes the importance of the temples as the chief centres for the use of the national script and as 'les dépositaires d'une civilisation intacte'.

13. An interesting Demotic papyrus containing part of the Egyptian code was discovered in 1938–9 on the site of the ancient Hermopolis; for a summary account of it see G. Mattha, 'A Preliminary Report on the Legal Code of Hermopolis West', in *Bull. de l'Inst. d'Égypte*, xxiii, 1941, pp. 297–312.

14. P. Tebt. i. 5. 207–20.

15. So E. Kiessling, 'Streiflichter zur Katökenfrage', in *Actes du Ve Congrès International de Papyrologie*, 1938, 213–29 (see pp. 215 ff.).

16. K. Sethe, J. Partsch, *Demotische Urkunden zum ägyptischen Bürgschaftsrecht* (Abh. der Phil.-Hist. Klasse der Sächs. Akad. der Wiss. xxxii, 1920), no. 7, p. 129. This document is dated in 202 B.C.

17. W. W. Tarn, *Hellenistic Civilisation*, 2nd ed., 1930, p. 164.

18. For Zênôn and his papers see, *inter alia*, M. Rostovtzeff, *A Large Estate in Egypt in the Third Century B.C.* (University of Wisconsin Studies, No. 6), Madison, 1922; H. I. Bell, 'A Greek Adventurer in Egypt', in *Edinburgh Review*, ccxliii, 1926, pp. 123–38 (a review of the preceding); C. C. Edgar's Introduction to P. Mich. I; V. Tscherikower, 'Palestine under the Ptolemies (A Contribution to the Study of the Zenon Papyri)', in *Mizraim*, iv–v, 1937, pp. 9–90; Claire Préaux, *Les Grecs en Égypte d'après les archives de Zénon*, Brussels, 1947.

19. In an unpublished Zenon papyrus in the British Museum.

20. Athenaeus v. 200 f-201.

21. P. Cairo Zen. 59157.

22. For banks in Egypt see: F. Preisigke, *Girowesen im griechischen Ägypten*, Strasbourg, 1910; J. Desvernos, 'Banques et Banquiers dans l'Égypte Ancienne', in *Bull. Soc. Roy. d'Arch. d'Alexandrie*, no. 23, 1928, pp. 303 ff.

23. Rostovtzeff, *Hellenistic World*, p. 406, leaves the question open.

24. W. W. Tarn, *Hellenistic Civilisation*, 2nd ed., p. 167.

25. Tarn, op. cit., p. 161, thinks that Alexander did not found 'a "city", a *polis*'; 'his foundations were probably of a new mixed type'. It seems extremely hazardous to assume this with no real evidence.

26. Rostovtzeff, *Hellenistic World*, pp. 927 ff., holds that the monsoon was discovered not in the Roman period but during the reign of Ptolemy Euergetês II (145–107 B.C.), but his arguments do not seem to me to outweigh those on the other side.

27. The site seems now clearly to have been identified; see, e.g., *Journ. of Hell. Studies*, lxv, 1945, pp. 106–8. Plaques found among the foundation deposits show that the builder was Ptolemy III; but his can hardly have been the first foundation.

28. The talent contained 6,000 drachmae. At the present rate of sterling the silver value of a talent may perhaps be reckoned at about £400.

29. For a recent article on Aristarchus see M. Meyerhof, 'Aristarque de Samos', in *Bull. de l'Inst. d'Égypte*, xxv, 1943, pp. 269–74.

30. In an able and interesting article, 'The Ptolemies and the Welfare of Their Subjects', in *Actes du Ve Congrès International de Papyrologie*, pp. 565–79 (see also *Am. Hist. Rev.* xliii, 1938, pp. 270–87), W. L. Westermann argues, against some very severe criticisms of Ptolemaic rule, that the Ptolemies did show thought and care for the welfare of the Egyptians and that the hostility of the latter towards the dynasty has been much exaggerated. He is certainly right in deprecating a too absolute condemnation of the régime, which on the whole compares favourably with Roman rule, but he is perhaps too favourable to it.

31. Thus Theocritus compares it with the brother-sister marriage of Olympian deities: 'He and that his fine noble spouse, who maketh him a better wife than ever clasped bridegroom under any roof, seeing that she loveth with her whole heart brother and husband in one. So too in heaven was the holy wedlock accomplished by those whom august Rhea bare to be rulers of Olympus, so too the myrrh-cleansed hands of the ever-maiden Iris lay but one couch for the slumbering of Zeus and Hera' (*Id.* xvii. 128–34, transl. by J. M. Edmonds). For the naming of a series of streets at Alexandria after Arsinoê, identified in each case with some Greek goddess, see H. I. Bell, *Archiv*, vii, 1924, pp. 21–4.

32. From E. Bevan's translation of Spiegelberg's German rendering (*Egypt under the Ptol. Dynasty*, pp. 388–9).

33. A more favourable view of Philopatôr is taken by Tarn (*Cambridge Ancient History*, vii, p. 727) than by Bevan (*Egypt under the Ptol. Dynasty*, pp. 220 ff.), but I confess I do not find his arguments convincing. There may well be exaggeration in the tradition, and Polybius may have been prejudiced against the king (though this is hardly proved), but the murders of Ptolemy's mother and his brother Magas are facts, and they must have been sanctioned, if they were not instigated, by him, and while it is very possible that the neglect of army and fleet began in the later days of Ptolemy III, it is quite clear that no attempt was made by Philopatôr or his ministers to remedy this until disaster threatened. The shameful treatment of his sister-wife, Arsinoê, is equally clear. A king must be judged in part by the character of his favourites and associates, and the reputation of Philopatôr's boon companions is beyond repair. History has many examples to prove that aesthetic sensibility and even a genuine religious feeling, both of which Philopatôr certainly had (for his edict on the cult of Dionysus see B.G.U. vi. 1211 and the references there), can coexist with moral degeneracy. J. Tondriau, 'Les thiases royaux de la cour Ptolémaïque', *Chron. d'Égypte*, xxi, no. 41, pp. 149–71, argues that the drinking parties and other feasts· recorded of Philopatôr and other rulers of the house were not mere debauchery but part of a deliberate policy and semi-religious in character; but even if he is right, Philopatôr's revels cannot have been of a very reputable kind; see, for example, the flash of scornful indignation recorded of Arsinoê by Eratosthenês, Philopatôr's tutor, in a passage quoted by Athenaeus (vii. 276 *b–c*): 'Arsinoe asked the man who was carrying the branches what day he was celebrating now, and what festival it was. He replied, "It is called the Feast of Flagons; the guests recline on beds of rushes and dine off the provisions they have carried with them, and every one drinks from his own flagon which he has brought from his own house." When he had gone she looked at us and said, "It seems a squalid sort of party; it must be a very mixed crowd, all of them served with stale food of the most unbecoming kind!" ' All we can really say on behalf of Philopatôr is that his policy may have had a coherence which the traditional picture of him ignores.

34. Cf. Cl. Préaux, 'Un problème de la politique des Lagides :

la faiblesse des édits', in *Atti del IV Congresso Internazionale di Papirologia*, 1936, pp. 183–93.

35. See Cl. Préaux, 'La Signification de l'époque d'Evergète II', in *Actes du Ve Congrès International de Papyrologie*, pp. 345–54. For periods of inflation see F. Heichelheim, *Wirtschaftliche Schwankungen der Zeit von Alexander bis Augustus*, Jena, 1930.

36. P. Tebt. iii. 698. For the date of these events see now Eric G. Turner, *Bull. of the John Rylands Library*, xxxi, 1948, pp. 4–6.

37. *Cambridge Ancient History*, x, p. 111.

38. *Journ. of Rom. Stud.* xxii, 1932, pp. 135–60. H. Fuchs, *Der geistige Widerstand gegen Rom in der antiken Welt* (Berlin, 1938), p. 36, rejects Tarn's view (cf. F. Oertel, *Klassenkampf, Sozialismus und organischer Staat im alten Griechenland*, Bonn, 1942, p. 63 note 133); but he makes no serious attempt to traverse Tarn's arguments, which, though they do not amount to demonstration, are very cogent.

39. See, e.g., W. Spiegelberg, 'Weshalb wählte Kleopatra den Tod durch Schlangenbiss?' in *Ägyptologische Mitteilungen* (Sitzungsber. der Bayerischen Akademie, 1925, Abh. 2, no. 1). Spiegelberg, by a curious slip, identifies the asp or uraeus (*naja haje*) with the horned viper (p. 5), but the *naja haje* is the cobra, though the south European viper is called *vipera aspis*. Bevan (*Egypt under the Ptol. Dynasty*, p. 382²) correctly speaks of a cobra.

CHAPTER III

1. Chiefly to the Juridicus. The Archidicastês may also have exercised some independent judicial functions, as, in matters affecting their own departments, did the *Dioikêtês*, a financial official, and the *Idios Logos*. For the prefect see O. W. Reinmuth, 'The Prefect of Egypt from Augustus to Diocletian' (*Klio*, Neue Folge, 21. Beiheft), Leipzig, 1935.

2. 'Beiträge zur antiken Urkundengeschichte', in *Archiv*, viii, pp. 216–39. Bickermann's thesis is not so convincing as regards the Ptolemaic period.

3. On the poll-tax see my recent article, 'The *Constitutio Antoniniana* and the Egyptian Poll-Tax', in *Journ. of Rom. Studies*, xxxvii, 1947, pp. 17–23.

4. On the municipal magistrates and their method of election see A. H. M. Jones, 'The Election of the Metropolitan Magistrates in Egypt', in *Journ. Eg. Arch.* xxiv, pp. 65–72. For the gymnasiarch see the monograph of B. A. van Groningen, *Le*

gymnasiarque des métropoles de l'Égypte romaine, Groningen, Noordhoff, 1924.

5. It is disputed whether such returns were compulsory. Registration of death could safely be left to the family concerned, since liability to poll-tax continued as long as a taxpayer's name remained on the taxing lists, but there was no such motive for making a return of birth, at least for the unprivileged, and compulsion is more likely there. But this is not certain.

6. There is an extensive literature dealing with these offices, especially the *bibliothêkê enktêseôn*; see the bibliography to chapter x of the *Cambridge Ancient History*, vol. x, pp. 927–8, 'The Document', especially the works by Eger, Lewald, Preisigke, and von Woess.

7. See, however, note 26 on Chapter II.

8. xvii. 788.

9. It is not quite fair to the Romans to write, as does Rostovtzeff, *Cambridge Ancient History*, vii, p. 154, 'Here and there in the edicts of certain emperors this note [of sympathy for the population of Egypt] is heard, but apart from that we pass, with the advent of the Roman governors, to a régime in which the voice of sympathy is dumb.' Quite apart from 'certain emperors' (notably Hadrian) we do find here and there, in the utterances of prefects or others, traces of humanitarian sentiment. Very striking is the way in which the prefect Titianus, 'in accordance not with the inhumanity of the law but with the choice of the daughter', set aside an old Egyptian law which gave a father power to take away his daughter from her husband (P. Oxy. ii. 237, vii. 34 f.). The legality of the father's claim was indisputable; the prefect acted on the principle of equity because he held the law to be inhumane (*apanthrôpos*). On the whole, however, Roman rule was marked, financially and administratively, by an unimaginative exploitation.

10. SB. 7462.

11. P. Tebt. ii. 327 = W. *Chrest.* 394.

12. *De Spec. Leg.* ii. 92 ff., iii. 159 ff.

13. P. Oxy. ii. 284; 285; 393; 394.

14. SB. 7462.

15. P. Fouad 8 is an interesting, though unfortunately very imperfect, record of the manifestations at Alexandria in favour of Vespasian; the prefect is mentioned in ll. 17, 18, probably also in l. 2.

16. See H. I. Bell, 'The Economic Crisis in Egypt under Nero', in *Journ. of Rom. Studies*, xxviii, pp. 1–8.

17. This is certainly suggested, e.g., by P. Harris 64, but since the salary mentioned is that of a deputy the evidence of this document is not conclusive. For the liturgy in general see F. Oertel, *Die Liturgie*, Leipzig, 1917.

18. See note 19 to Chap. IV.

19. See, e.g., H. I. Bell, 'An Epoch in the Agrarian History of Egypt', in *Recueil Champollion*, Paris, 1922, pp. 261–71.

20. P. Oxy. xviii. 2192. The translations are those of the editor. Hypsicrates' work is unrecorded elsewhere, nor was Thersagoras known previously. See also H. I. Bell, 'The "Thyestes" of Sophocles and an Egyptian Scriptorium', in *Aegyptus*, ii, pp. 281–8; in the account of a book-shop from which extracts are there published are mentioned, besides the third *Thyestes*, the *Plutus* of Aristophanes and other works. The whole fragment, probably from Oxyrhynchus, is published by K. Ohly, *Stichometrische Untersuchungen* (Leipzig, 1928), pp. 88–9. For the range of literature available at Oxyrhynchus see Sir F. G. Kenyon, 'The Library of a Greek of Oxyrhynchus', in *Journ. Eg. Arch.* viii, pp. 129–38. The list given in this article could now be extended. C. H. Oldfather, *The Greek Literary Texts from Greco-Roman Egypt*, Madison, 1923, gives a list of the literary works then available in papyri or ostraca. This list is continued and brought up to date by the recent work of L. Giallani, *Testi letterari greci di provenienza egiziana* (1920–45), Florence, 1946.

21. For example *a di kos ê the os* (*adikos hê theos*), &c., O. Guéraud, P. Jouguet, *Un livre d'écolier du IIIᵉ siècle avant J.-C.*, Cairo, 1938, p. 14, l. 121.

22. P. Oxy. vi. 930 = *Select Papyri*, i, no. 130.

23. P. Giss. 85.

24. By Oldfather, op. cit., pp. 68 ff.

25. P. Oxy. xviii. 2190. The translation is again that of the editor.

26. P. Oxy. iv. 724 (= *Select Papyri*, i, no. 15) is an apprenticeship to a shorthand writer for a period of two years. For Greek shorthand see, e.g., H. J. M. Milne, *Greek Shorthand Manuals*, London, 1934; A. Mentz, 'Beiträge zur hellenistischen Tachygraphie', in *Archiv*, xi, pp. 64–73.

27. P. Lond. iii. 1178 = W. *Chrest.* 156 is a diploma of membership in 'The Sacred Athletic Peripatetic Hadrianian Antoninian Septimian Association of the Votaries of Heracles', the chief athletic club of the Empire, issued at Naples in A.D. 194 to a boxer of Hermopolis in Egypt.

28. P. Oxy. iii. 413 contains both a farce and a mime, no doubt performed locally, and there are several other examples.

29. On this subject see, e.g., Teresa Grassi, 'Musica, Mimica e Danza', in *Studî della Scuola Papirologica*, Milan, iii, 1920, pp. 117–35.

30. P. Brem. 63.

31. P. Amh. 70, 2–4: 'His excellency the prefect Rutilius Lupus having ordered that the burden of the expenses of the gymnasiarchy be reduced in order that those nominated should more readily undertake the expense.' This indicates that it was already becoming difficult to obtain suitable candidates, but that it was still possible to refuse nomination. The date of Lupus' prefecture was A.D. 113 (or 114)–117.

32. A papyrus published by K. S. Gapp, *Trans. Am. Phil. Ass.* lxiv, 1933, pp. 89–97, suggests that this privilege was abrogated about A.D. 254–5; see too E. P. Wegener, *Symbolae van Oven*, Leyden, 1946, p. 182, note 117. For the existence of the privilege see P. Oxy. viii. 1119 = W. *Chrest.* 397, 16, and for Antinoopolis and its status and privileges generally see H. I. Bell, 'Antinoopolis: A Hadrianic Foundation in Egypt', in *Journ. of Rom. Studies*, xxx, 1940, pp. 133–47.

33. P. Oxy. iii. 473 = W. *Chrest.* 33.

34. P. Ryl. ii. 77 (A.D. 192) is an instructive and (for the modern reader) amusing account of the nomination of a *cosmêtês* and the desperate but unsuccessful attempts of the man nominated to escape the burden.

35. P. Oxy. iv. 705 = W. *Chrest.* 407.

36. On this subject see H. I. Bell, 'Evidences of Christianity in Egypt during the Roman Period', in *Harv. Theol. Rev.* xxxvii, 1944, pp. 185–208.

37. P. Ryl. iii. 457. Published separately by C. H. Roberts, *An Unpublished Fragment of the Fourth Gospel*, Manchester, 1935.

38. *Apol.* xl.

39. This, for example, is how St. Perpetua (to whose hand we owe the first part of the narrative, continued by one of her fellow martyrs, and completed after the martyrdom by a third writer) tells the story of her examination: 'We arrived at the Forum. At once the news spread through the districts adjoining the Forum, and a huge crowd gathered. We went up to the tribunal. The others were interrogated and confessed. My turn came, and my father thereupon appeared with my son, and drew me from the dock, imploring me: "Have pity on your infant child." And

Hilarianus, the procurator, who had at that time, on the death of the proconsul Minucius Timinianus, taken over the power of life and death, said: "Spare your father's gray hairs; spare the infancy of your boy; sacrifice for the preservation of the Emperors." And I replied: "I will not." Hilarianus said: "Are you a Christian?" and I replied: "I am a Christian." And when my father was about to drag me down Hilarion ordered him to be dragged down, and he struck him with a staff. And I was as grieved for my father's misfortune as if I had been struck myself; so did I grieve for his unhappy old age. Then he [the procurator] passed sentence on all of us, and condemned us to be thrown to the beasts; and we went down joyfully to the prison' (J. Armitage Robinson, *Texts and Studies*, vol. i, no. 2, 'The Passion of S. Perpetua', Cambridge, 1891, p. 70). Cf. ibid., 'Acts of the Scillitan Martyrs', p. 114: 'Saturninus, the proconsul, said: "Have no part in this madness." Cittinus said: "We have none other to fear except the Lord our God, who is in Heaven." Donata said: "Honour to Caesar as Caesar; but fear to God." Vestia said: "I am a Christian." Secunda said: "What I am, even that I desire to be." Saturninus, the proconsul, said to Speratus: "Do you persevere in your Christianity?" Speratus said: "I am a Christian." And with him all agreed.'

40. See J. R. Knipfing, 'The Libelli of the Decian Persecution', in *Harv. Theol. Rev.* xvi, 1923, pp. 345–90.

41. See J. N. Sanders, *The Fourth Gospel in the Early Church*, Cambridge, 1943.

42. See P. N. Harrison, *Polycarp's Two Epistles to the Philippians*, Cambridge, 1936, pp. 257, 302 ff. I cannot agree with Harrison in thinking that St. John was not published till about A.D. 135.

43. W. *Chrest.* 14 (made up of B.G.U. ii. 511 and P. Cairo 10448).

44. H. I. Bell, 'A New Fragment of the Acta Isidori', in *Archiv*, x, pp. 5–16 (l. 18 of the papyrus).

45. P. Oxy. x. 1242, 52 ff.

46. P. Oxy. i. 33 (= W. *Chrest.* 20), 3–7. For anti-Semitism at Alexandria see, e.g.: U. Wilcken, 'Zum alexandrinischen Antisemitismus', in *Abhandl. d. Kön. Sächs. Gesellsch. d. Wissensch.*, phil.-hist. Kl. xxvii, pp. 783–839; A. von Premerstein, 'Zu den sogenannten alexandrinischen Märtyrerakten', in *Philologus*, Supplementband xvi, Heft 11; H. I. Bell, *Juden und Griechen im römischen Alexandreia* (Beihefte zum 'Alten Orient', Heft 9), Leipzig, 1926; 'Anti-semitism at Alexandria', in *Journ. of Rom. Studies*, xxxi, 1941, pp. 1–18.

47. Eusebius, *Hist. eccles.* vii. 32. 5. See Norman H. Baynes, *The Thought-World of East Rome*, Oxford, 1947, p. 26.

48. *Protrept.* x.

49. 'When he [Theodore of Sykeon] emerged from the cave, the bishop of Anastasioupolis in Galatia Prima was present, and when the bishop saw the pus oozing from the sores on Theodore's body, when he saw the indescribable number of worms in his matted hair, when he experienced the intolerable stench which made Theodore unapproachable, the bishop was so convinced of Theodore's holiness that on the spot he ordained him lector, sub-deacon, deacon, and priest' (Baynes, op. cit., p. 17).

50. See E. G. Turner, 'Egypt and the Roman Empire: The δεκάπρωτοι', in *Journ. Eg. Arch.* xxii, 1936, pp. 7–19; E. P. Wegener, *Symbolae van Oven*, Leyden, 1946, pp. 167–72. Miss Wegener's article, 'The βουλευταί of the μητροπόλεις in Roman Egypt' (pp. 160–90), is of the first importance for the senates and municipal magistracies.

51. See, on this subject, Wegener, op. cit., pp. 171 ff. She concludes, no doubt rightly, from P. Lond. Inv. no. 2565, 69–74 (see note 55) that there was no distinction in the matter of property qualification between the magistrates (*archontes*) and ordinary senators. But that papyrus refers to the middle of the third century. It does not necessarily follow that when the senates were created no persons not previously liable to compulsion to the *honores* were enrolled. In any case, whereas a magistrate was burdened by the expenses of his office only while he held it, a senator was responsible as guarantor for officials nominated to *munera* and perhaps for other charges even when he was not himself holding office.

52. See, e.g., C.P.R. 20 = W. *Chrest.* 402.

53. An excellent characterization of the period is given by Claire Préaux, 'Sur le déclin de l'Empire au iiie siècle de notre ère', in *Chron. d'Égypte*, xvi, no. 31, 1941, pp. 123–31.

54. P. Oxy. x. 1252 verso.

55. T. C. Skeat and E. P. Wegener, 'A Trial before the Prefect of Egypt Appius Sabinus, *c.* 250 A.D.', in *Journ. Eg. Arch.* xxi, 1935, pp. 224–47. If, as seems probable (cf. note 32 above), the privilege of the Antinoopolites was abolished about 254–5, that fact is also very significant of the position in the nome-capitals.

56. On the crown tax see S. L. Wallace, *Taxation in Egypt*, pp. 281–4; H. I. Bell, *Journ. Rom. Studies*, xxxvii, p. 20.

57. Cf. Claire Préaux, *Actes du Ve Congrès Intern. de Papyrologie*, p. 348: 'Dans un pays très peuplé, lorsque l'éclosion de la propriété privée est due à un accroissement du pouvoir économique de l'individu, à un développement intense des échanges, on voit le terroir se diviser à l'extrême, en petites propriétés. Au contraire, si l'épanouissement de l'individualisme juridique ne porte ses fruits qu'au moment où la vie économique se rétrécit, la terre, libérée de la main du roi, va nécessairement passer aux seuls individus qui possèdent quelque puissance économique.'

58. The chief published collection of these papyri will be found in P. Flor. ii. A Belgian scholar, Dr. J. Bingen, is at present engaged on a study of the Hêrôninus papers, including some unpublished documents in the British Museum and elsewhere.

59. P. Flor. ii. 127 = *Select Papyri*, i, no. 140.

60. The *capitatio* and *iugatio* are subjects beset with difficulties and much disputed among historians. For Diocletian's reforms see W. Ensslin, 'The Reforms of Diocletian', in *Cambridge Ancient History*, xii, chap. xi. See now, too, W. Seston, *Dioclétien et la Tétrarchie*, Paris, 1946.

61. A. E. R. Boak, 'Early Byzantine Papyri from the Cairo Museum', no. 1, in *Études de Papyrologie*, ii, 1934, pp. 1–8.

CHAPTER IV

1. See above, p. 99.

2. See N. H. Baynes, *Cambridge Ancient History*, vol. xii, p. 668 and references.

3. *Apol.* l, 'Plures efficimur quoties metimur a vobis: semen est sanguis Christianorum' ('We grow in numbers, as often as we are mown down by you: the blood of Christians is our seed').

4. See N. H. Baynes, 'Constantine the Great and the Christian Church' in *Proc. of Brit. Acad.* xv, 1929, p. 347.

5. *Inferno*, xix. 115–17.

6. 'Godhead was one; there were many telephone lines and they ran through a number, smaller but appreciable, of different switchboards'; A. D. Nock, *Journ. of Rom. Studies*, xxxvii, 1947, p. 104.

7. A papyrus in the British Museum (P. Lond. 1914), a letter from a Melitian at Alexandria to a fellow schismatic, gives a vivid picture of Athanasius' proceedings against the Melitians ('he carried off a Bishop of the Lower Country and shut him in the Meat Market, and a priest of the same region he shut in the lock-

up, and a deacon in the principal prison, and till the twenty-eighth of Pachon Heraiscus too [probably an Alexandrian 'anti-pope' set up by the Melitians as a rival to Athanasius] has been confined in the Camp—I thank God our Master that the scourgings which he endured have ceased—and on the twenty-seventh he caused seven Bishops to leave the country') and his irresolution when summoned by Constantine to the Synod of Tyre in A.D. 335 ('Athanasius is very despondent. Often (?) did they come for him, and till now he has not left the country; but he had his baggage embarked at sea as though he would leave the country, and then again he took his baggage off the ship, not wishing to leave the country'). See H. I. Bell, *Jews and Christians in Egypt*, 1924, p. 62. For a popular account of St. Athanasius see H. I. Bell, 'Athanasius: A Chapter in Church History', in *The Congregational Quarterly*, iii, 1925, pp. 158–76.

8. See Wilcken's discussion of this in UPZ. i, pp. 52–77.

9. It is, however, to be noted that the custom was mainly found in the Hellenic Sarapis cult, and that the majority of the *katochoi* known to us were Greeks or Macedonians. It may, on the other hand, be pointed out that the word *anachôrêtês* from which our 'anchorite' comes recalls the *anachôrêsis*, or flight, which from time immemorial had been the last resource of the Egyptian peasant when his position became intolerable.

10. 'The Garden of Ptolemagrius at Panopolis', in *Trans. Am. Phil. Ass.* lxxvii, 1946, pp. 192–206. Mr. Roberts points out that the 'Garden' of Epicurus is perhaps a likelier influence than anything Egyptian.

11. See L. Keimer, 'L'Horreur des Égyptiens pour les démons du désert', in *Bull. de l'Inst. d'Égypte*, xxvi, 1943–4, pp. 135–47.

12. P. Jews (= P. Lond.) 1923–9.

13. P. Jews 1923.

14. P. Jews 1926.

15. P. Jews 1928.

16. P. Jews 1929.

17. P. Cairo Masp. iii. 67295. See i. 12–16, 18–20: 'I may say, if it be not reprehensible to praise oneself, that I have for long enjoyed no small reputation among the inhabitants of the great city of Alexander; for conducting a school in the university there I always observed a right standard of living and, zealously practising my innate faculty for intellectual pursuits, imparted an education in philosophy to those who desired it; this being indeed

an interest inherited from my parents and grandparents, for I
had as my instructor my thrice blessed father Asclêpiadês, who
laboured all his life in the Museums, instructing the young according to the ancient curriculum. . . . In the same city I was eager
to observe a similar way of life. . . . My wife, who is also my cousin,
and myself were the children of two brothers, I and she, and our
fathers lived together, never parted the one from the other,
whether in his interests, in his domicile, in uprightness, or in
devotion to the muse of philosophy, so that many doubted of
which parents we came, whether I was the son of her father or she
the daughter of mine.' The writer is Hôrapollôn, the author of
a work on the antiquities of Alexandria and probably of the extant
treatise on hieroglyphics mentioned in the text.

18. See E. P. Wegener, *Symbolae van Oven*, p. 173, for conditions
in the third century: 'We may draw the conclusion that in Egypt
the function of senator was hereditary probably already in the
third century for those who belonged to the archons at least.'

19. A. E. R. Boak, 'An Egyptian Farmer of the Age of Diocletian and Constantine', in *Byzantina Metabyzantina*, i, 1946,
pp. 39–53, sums up his study of a collection of papyri from
Theadelphia in the Fayyûm as follows: 'From the foregoing study
of the career of Isidoros and its comparison with that of Sakaon,
two conclusions of some significance can be drawn. One, that, as
intimated above, agriculture in the Fayum in the early fourth
century could still be made a profitable occupation, provided that
the irrigation services could be maintained. Since these failed at
Theadelphia, agriculture was doomed and the site was abandoned
by its inhabitants. But at Karanis the canals continued to function
and the community survived for another century. Secondly, that
the village landholders must reconcile themselves to holding some
six or more different liturgical offices, some for more than one
term, during their maturer years. This surely was a burden heavy
enough in times of prosperity, but when added to the load of
taxation in a period when the cost of government was draining the
resources of the provinces to the point of exhaustion, it is not surprising that in the long run it proved an intolerable load. The
career of Isidoros lends new emphasis to the generally accepted
opinion that the liturgical system was largely responsible for the
ruin of the propertied class in the towns and villages of Egypt in the
early Byzantine period.' Of course the financial burden and the
consequent flight of those whom it ruined, by reducing available

man-power, made it more difficult to maintain the irrigation system, and its neglect in turn accentuated the financial strain.

20. This is a probable inference from the fact that the village of Aphrodite was granted the right of *autopragia* by the Emperor Leo (P. Cairo Masp. i. 67019, 5 f.) and the statement by the villagers in a petition dating from A.D. 567 that the pagarchy of Antaeopolis had up till then had eight pagarchs (P. Cairo Masp. i. 67002, ii, 18 f.).

21. For this date, in preference to 538, hitherto usually accepted, see Gertrude Malz, 'The Date of Justinian's Edict XIII', in *Byzantion*, xvi, 1942–3, pp. 135–41.

22. A tentative genealogy of the family is given in P. Oxy. xvi. 1829, 24, note (p. 6); E. R. Hardy, *Large Estates*, p. 38.

23. P. Oxy. xvi. 1982.

24. See P. Oxy. xvi. 1928, introd.

25. This was the case, for example, at Aphrodite, a free village possessing *autopragia* but containing also an estate of a noble named Ammônius; see *Journ. of Hell. Studies*, lxiv, p. 24.

26. P. Cairo Masp. i. 67002; P. Lond. v. 1674.

27. P. Cairo Masp. i. 67024, 15 f.

28. P. Hib. 34.

29. P. Oxy. i. 130.

30. P. Cairo Masp. i. 67002.

31. P. Oxy. xvi. 1860, 6.

32. P. Oxy. xvi. 1987.

33. Even the great Apiôn family was at one time monophysite; see Hardy, *Large Estates*, pp. 26–7.

34. See C. H. Roberts, 'A Latin Parchment from Antinoë', in *Aegyptus*, xv, 1935, pp. 297–302, especially p. 302. The text is published in *Journ. Eg. Arch.* xxi, 1935, pp. 199–209.

35. See H. I. Bell, 'An Egyptian Village in the Age of Justinian', in *Journ. of Hell. Studies*, lxiv, 1944, pp. 21–36; J. Maspero, 'Un dernier poète grec d'Égypte: Dioscore fils d'Apollos', in *Rev. des études grecques*, xxiv, 1911, pp. 426–81; H. J. M. Milne, *Cat. of the Literary Papyri in the British Museum*, 1927, pp. 68–80; H. I. Bell and W. E. Crum, 'A Greek-Coptic Glossary', in *Aegyptus*, vi, 1925, pp. 177–226.

36. P. Lond. i. 77 (pp. 231–36) = M. *Chrest.* 319.

37. Cf. my remarks in W. E. Crum and H. I. Bell, *Wadi Sarga*, Copenhagen, 1922, pp. 16–18.

38. See J. Maspero, *Org. militaire*, pp. 114–18.

39. See A. J. Butler, *The Treaty of Miṣr in Ṭabarī*, Oxford, 1913.

BIBLIOGRAPHY

GENERAL

THE following general works, covering the whole Graeco-Roman period, with a special view to the papyrus evidence, can be recommended:

SCHUBART (Wilhelm), *Ägypten von Alexander dem Grossen bis auf Mohammed*. Berlin, Weidmann, 1922. [A general survey of life and conditions in Egypt, arranged topographically, in three parts: Alexandria, Memphis and the Fayyûm, the Thebaid.]

WINTER (J. G.), *Life and Letters in the Papyri*, Ann Arbor, University of Michigan Press, 1933. [Does not require any knowledge of Greek, though quotations in Greek are included.]

DEISSMANN (Adolf), *Light from the Ancient East*. Transl. from the German by L. R. M. Strachan. New edition, London, Hodder and Stoughton, 1927. [Deals with inscriptions and archaeological discoveries in all the Nearer East but includes the texts, with translations, of many papyri and some ostraca from Egypt.]

SCHUBART (Wilhelm), *Ein Jahrtausend am Nil*. Second edition, Berlin, Weidmann, 1923. [Translations into German of 101 letters, chiefly on papyrus, chosen to illustrate life in Graeco-Roman Egypt at various periods, with an informative introduction and comments on each letter.]

MEECHAM (H. G.), *Light from Ancient Letters: Private Correspondence in the Non-literary Papyri of Oxyrhynchus of the First Four Centuries and its Bearing on New Testament Language and Thought*. London, Allen and Unwin, 1923.

PREISIGKE (Friedrich), *Antikes Leben nach den ägyptischen Papyri*. Leipzig, Teubner, 1916.

BELL (H. I.), 'Hellenic Culture in Egypt', in *Journal of Egyptian Archaeology*, viii, pp. 139–155.

JOUGUET (P.), 'Les Destinées de l'hellénisme dans l'Égypte gréco-romaine', in *Chronique d'Égypte*, x, 1935, no. 19, pp. 89–108.

SCHUBART (Wilhelm), *Die Griechen in Ägypten*. (Beihefte zum 'Alten Orient', Heft 10.) Leipzig, Hinrichs, 1927.

ROBERTS (C. H.), 'The Greek Papyri', chapter x of *The Legacy of Egypt* (Oxford, 1942).

Hunt (A. S.) and Edgar (C. C.), *Select Papyri*, 2 vols. London, Heinemann (Loeb Classical Library), 1932, 1934. [A selection of representative papyrus texts of all periods with English translations and occasional explanatory notes.]

CHAPTER I

1. General Works on Papyrology

Mitteis (L.) und Wilcken (U.), *Grundzüge und Chrestomathie der Papyruskunde*. Leipzig–Berlin, Teubner, 1912. [The standard and indispensable work of reference for any thorough study of Greek papyri. In two volumes, each in two parts, respectively *Grundzüge* and *Chrestomathie*. [**W. Chrest., M. Chrest.** are the standard abbreviations for texts in the latter.] Vol. i, by Wilcken, deals with papyrology as a science, with history, racial elements and conflicts, religion, education, finance and taxation, administration, industry and trade, agriculture, the postal and transport system, military and police, and social life. Vol. ii, by Mitteis, is devoted to the legal systems and institutions of Graeco-Roman Egypt. The texts edited in the second part of each volume illustrate the sketch given in the first part.]

Schubart (Wilhelm), *Einführung in die Papyruskunde*. Berlin, Weidmann, 1918. [A valuable supplement to Mitteis–Wilcken, dealing not only with the subjects treated by them but also with literary and Christian papyri; with copious references but without illustrative texts.]

Preisendanz (Karl), *Papyrusfunde und Papyrusforschung*. Leipzig, Hiersemann, 1933.

Calderini (Aristide), *Manuale di Papirologia antica greca e romana ad uso delle scuole universitarie e delle persone colte*. Milan, Ceschina, 1938.

Peremans (W.) en Vergote (J.), *Papyrologisch Handboek*. Louvain, Beheer van Philologische Studiën, 1942. [The latest comprehensive handbook of papyrology, written in Flemish. There are full bibliographies to each chapter. The last two chapters, on culture and morality and on private life, were not written, and only the bibliographies are given.]

David (M.) and van Groningen (B. A.), *Papyrological Primer*. Second (English) edition, Leyden, Brill, 1946. [A collection of well-chosen and well-edited papyrus texts, 85 in number, selected to initiate students into the study of papyrology in its various aspects and preceded by an introduction which gives a summary but very useful survey of the subject.]

2. PRINCIPAL EDITIONS OF GREEK PAPYRI AND OSTRACA

A. *Papyri* (*with the standard methods of reference*)

B.G.U. = *Aegyptische Urkunden aus den Staatlichen Museen zu Berlin, Griechische Urkunden.* Berlin, 1895, &c. At present 8 vols.

B.K.T. = *Berliner Klassikertexte.* Berlin, 1904, &c. Literary texts in the Berlin papyri. At present 8 vols.

C. P. Herm. = *Stud. Pal.* v (see below): *Corpus Papyrorum Hermopolitanorum.*

C.P.R. = *Corpus Papyrorum Raineri,* i, by C. Wessely. Vienna, 1895.

M. Chrest. = Mitteis, *Chrestomathie.*

P. Aberd. = *Catalogue of Greek and Latin Papyri and Ostraca in the Possession of the University of Aberdeen,* by E. G. Turner. Aberdeen, 1939.

P. Achmîm = *Les Papyrus grecs d'Achmîm,* by P. Collart. Cairo, 1930.

P. Adler = *The Adler Papyri,* Greek texts by E. N. Adler, J. G. Tait, and F. M. Heichelheim, Demotic by F. Ll. Griffith. Oxford, 1939.

P. Amh. = *The Amherst Papyri . . . of . . . Lord Amherst of Hackney,* by B. P. Grenfell and A. S. Hunt. London, 1900, 1901.

P. Amst. See **P. Gron.**

P. Bacchias = 'The Archives of the Temple of Soknobraisis at Bacchias', by Elizabeth H. Gilliam. *Yale Classical Studies,* x, 1947, pp. 181–281.

P. Baden = *Veröffentlichungen aus den badischen Papyrus-Sammlungen.* Heidelberg, 1923, &c. Demotic, Coptic, and Greek texts, edited by W. Spiegelberg, F. Bilabel, and G. A. Gerhard, are included. At present 6 parts.

P. Bas. = *Papyrusurkunden der Öffentlichen Bibliothek der Universität zu Basel,* by E. Rabel and (one Coptic contract) W. Spiegelberg. Berlin, 1917.

P. Berl. Frisk = *Bankakten aus dem Faijûm nebst anderen Berliner Papyri,* by H. Frisk. Göteborg, 1931.

P. Berl. Leihg. = *Berliner Leihgabe griechischer Papyri,* by T. Kalén and the Greek Seminar of Uppsala. Uppsala, 1932.

P. Berl. Möller = *Griechische Papyri aus dem Berliner Museum,* by S. Möller. Göteborg, 1929.

P. Bour. = *Les Papyrus Bouriant,* by P. Collart. Paris, 1926.

154   *Bibliography*

P. Brem. = *Die Bremer Papyri* (Abhandlungen der Preussischen Akademie der Wissenschaften), by U. Wilcken. Berlin, 1936.

P. Cairo Masp. = *Catalogue général des antiquités égyptiennes du Musée du Caire; Papyrus grecs d'époque byzantine*, by J. Maspero. Cairo, 1911–16. 3 vols.

P. Cairo Preis. = *Griechische Urkunden des Ägyptischen Museums zu Kairo*, by F. Preisigke. Strassburg, 1911.

P. Cairo Zen. = *Catalogue général des antiquités égyptiennes du Musée du Caire; Zenon Papyri*, by C. C. Edgar. Cairo, 1925–31. 4 vols.; the series completed posthumously by vol. v, published by the Société Fouad I de Papyrologie and edited from Edgar's materials by O. Guéraud and P. Jouguet.

P. Col. Inv. 480 (P. Col. I) = *Upon Slavery in Ptolemaic Egypt*, by W. L. Westermann. New York, 1929.

P. Col. II = *Tax Lists and Transportation Receipts from Theadelphia*, by W. L. Westermann and C. W. Keyes. New York, 1932.

P. Col. Zen. = *Zenon Papyri: Business Papers of the Third Century B.C. dealing with Palestine and Egypt*. Vol. i by W. L. Westermann and E. S. Hasenoehrl, New York, 1934; vol. ii by W. L. Westermann, C. W. Keyes, and H. Liebesny, New York, 1940.

P. Cornell = *Greek Papyri in the Library of Cornell University*, by W. L. Westermann and C. J. Kraemer, Jr. New York, 1926.

P. Edfou = *Les Papyrus et les ostraca grecs*, by J. Manteuffel, being chapter v of *Fouilles franco-polonaises*, Rapport I, *Tell Edfou 1937*. Cairo, 1937.

P. Eleph. = *Elephantine-Papyri*, by O. Rubensohn. Berlin, 1907.

P. Ent. = *ENTEYΞEIΣ: Requêtes et plaintes adressées au roi d'Égypte au IIIᵉ siècle avant J.-C.*, by O. Guéraud. Cairo, 1931–2.

P. Erlangen = *Die Papyri der Universitätsbibliothek Erlangen*, by W. Schubart. Leipzig, 1942. [Published during the war, this volume may not have reached this country. The whole remaining stock appears to have perished in a bombardment. The present writer saw a copy at Brussels.]

P. Fay. = *Fayûm Towns and their Papyri*, by B. P. Grenfell, A. S. Hunt, and D. G. Hogarth. London, 1900.

P. Flor. = *Papiri greco-egizii*, by D. Comparetti and G. Vitelli. Milan, 1905–15. 3 vols.

P. Fouad = *Les Papyrus Fouad I* (Publ. de la Société Fouad I de Papyrologie, Textes et Documents, iii), by A. Bataille, O. Guéraud, P. Jouguet, and others. Cairo, 1939.

P. Frankf. = *Griechische Papyri aus dem Besitz des Rechtswissen-*

Bibliography 155

schaftlichen Seminars der Universität Frankfurt, by H. Lewald. Heidelberg, 1920.

P. Freib. = Mitteilungen aus der Freiburger Papyrussammlung, by W. Aly, M. Gelzer, J. Partsch, and U. Wilcken. Heidelberg, 1914–27. 3 Parts; Part III is in a larger size than the others.

P. Gen. = Les Papyrus de Genève, i, by J. Nicole. Geneva, 1896–1900.

P. Giss. = Griechische Papyri im Museum des oberhessischen Geschichtsvereins zu Giessen, by O. Eger, E. Kornemann, and P. M. Meyer. Leipzig–Berlin, 1910–12.

P. Giss. Univ.-Bibl. = Mitteilungen aus der Papyrussammlung der Giessener Universitätsbibliothek, by H. Kling and others. Giessen, 1924–39. 6 parts.

P.G.M. = Papyri Magicae Graecae, by K. Preisendanz. Leipzig–Berlin, 1928, 1931. 2 vols.

P. Got. = Papyrus grecs de la Bibliothèque Municipale de Gothembourg, by H. Frisk. Göteborg, 1929.

P. Grenf. I = An Alexandrian Erotic Fragment and other Greek Papyri chiefly Ptolemaic, by B. P. Grenfell. Oxford, 1896.

P. Grenf. II = New Classical Fragments and other Greek and Latin Papyri, by B. P. Grenfell and A. S. Hunt. Oxford, 1897.

P. Gron. = Papyri Groninganae: Griechische Papyri der Universitätsbibliothek zu Groningen nebst zwei Papyri der Universitätsbibliothek zu Amsterdam, by A. G. Roos. Amsterdam, 1933.

P. Gurob = Greek Papyri from Gurob, by J. G. Smyly. Dublin, 1921.

P. Hal. = Dikaiomata: Auszüge aus Alexandrinischen Gesetzen und Verordnungen in einem Papyrus des philologischen Seminars der Universität Halle mit einem Anhang weiterer Papyri derselben Sammlung, by the Graeca Halensis. Berlin, 1913.

P. Hamb. = Griechische Papyrusurkunden der Hamburger Staats- und Universitätsbibliothek, vol. i, by P. M. Meyer. Leipzig–Berlin, 1911–24.

P. Harris = The Rendel Harris Papyri of Woodbrooke College, Birmingham, by J. E. Powell. Cambridge, 1936.

P. Haun. = Papyri Graecae Haunienses, fasc. i, by T. Larsen. Copenhagen, 1942.

P. Hib. = The Hibeh Papyri, Part I, by B. P. Grenfell and A. S. Hunt. London, 1906.

P. Iand. = Papyri Iandanae, cum discipulis edidit C. Kalbfleisch. Leipzig, 1912, &c. At present 8 parts.

156   *Bibliography*

P. Jena = *Jenaer Papyrus-Urkunden,* by F. Zucker and F. Schneider. Jena, 1926.

P. Jews = *Jews and Christians in Egypt: The Jewish Troubles in Alexandria and the Athanasian Controversy,* by H. I. Bell. London, 1924.

P. kl. Form. = Parts III and VIII of *Stud. Pal.* (see below): *Griechische Papyrusurkunden kleineren Formats,* by C. Wessely.

P. Lille = *Papyrus grecs* (Institut Papyrologique de l'Université de Lille), by P. Jouguet, P. Collart, J. Lesquier, M. Xoual. Paris, 1907, 1912. 2 vols. [Vol. ii contains the papyri from Magdola in the Fayyûm, later re-edited by Guéraud in P. Ent.]

P. Lips. = *Griechische Urkunden der Papyrussammlung zu Leipzig,* vol. i, by L. Mitteis, Leipzig, 1906.

P. Lond. = *Greek Papyri in the British Museum,* by F. G. Kenyon and H. I. Bell. London, 1893–1917. At present 5 vols. [P. Jews continues the numerical sequence of the London papyri, but forms a separate publication.]

P. Lugd. Bat. = *Papyri Graeci Musei Antiquarii publici Lugduni-Batavi,* by C. Leemans. Leyden, 1843, 1885.

P. Lund Univ.-Bibl. = *Aus der Papyrussammlung der Universitätsbibliothek in Lund,* by A. Wifstrand, K. Hanell, and E. K. Knudtzon. Lund, 1935–46. At present 4 parts.

P. Magd. = P. Lille II.

P. Marmarica = *Il papiro Vaticano greco 11,* by M. Norsa and G. Vitelli. Città del Vaticano, 1931.

P. Meyer = *Griechische Texte aus Ägypten: I. Papyri des Neutestamentlichen Seminars der Universität Berlin, II. Ostraka der Sammlung Deissmann,* by P. M. Meyer. Berlin, 1916.

P. Mich. = *Papyri in the University of Michigan Collection,* by C. C. Edgar, A. E. R. Boak, J. G. Winter, and others. Ann Arbor, 1931–47. At present 7 vols. [Each volume has a sub-title of its own. The numerical sequence of volumes as a single series was not established till vol. iii. Vol. i, *Zenon Papyri,* by C. C. Edgar, is often referred to as **P. Mich. Zen.**]   [1928.

P. Mil. = *Papiri Milanesi,* vol. i, fasc. 1, by A. Calderini. Milan,

P. Mil. R. Univ. = *Papiri della R. Università di Milano,* Vol. Primo, by A. Vogliano. Milan, 1937. [Sometimes called **P. Primi,** to distinguish this from the other Milanese series.]

P. Monac. = *Veröffentlichungen aus der Papyrus-Sammlung der K. Hof- und Staatsbibliothek zu München: Byzantinische Papyri,* by A. Heisenberg and L. Wenger. Leipzig–Berlin, 1914.

P. Neutest. = P. Meyer.

P. Osl. = *Papyri Osloenses*, by S. Eitrem and L. Amundsen. Oslo, 1925–36. At present 3 vols.

P. Oxford = *Some Oxford Papyri*, by E. P. Wegener. Leyden, 1942. [Vol. iii of the series 'Papyrologica Lugduno-Batava'.]

P. Oxy. = *The Oxyrhynchus Papyri*, by B. P. Grenfell, A. S. Hunt, and others. 1898 ff. At present 18 vols.

P. Par. = *Notices et textes des papyrus grecs du Musée du Louvre et de la Bibliothèque Impériale* (Notices et Extraits des manuscrits de la Bibl. Impériale et autres Bibl. 18. 2), by Letronne and Brunet de Presle. Paris, 1865.

P. Petrie = *The Flinders Petrie Papyri*, by J. P. Mahaffy and J. G. Smyly. Dublin, 1891–1905. 3 vols.

P. Primi = P. Mil. R. Univ.

P. Princ. = *Papyri in the Princeton University Collections*, by A. C. Johnson, H. B. Van Hoesen, E. H. Kase, Jr., and S. P. Goodrich. Baltimore and Princeton, 1931–42. At present 3 vols.

P. Rein. = *Papyrus grecs et démotiques recueillis en Égypte*, by Th. Reinach, W. Spiegelberg, and S. de Ricci. Paris, 1905. *Les Papyrus Théodore Reinach*, t. ii, ed. P. Collart, &c. Cairo, 1940.

P. Rev. = *Revenue Laws of Ptolemy Philadelphus*, by B. P. Grenfell. Oxford, 1896.

P. Ross.-Georg. = *Papyri russischer und georgischer Sammlungen*, by G. Zereteli, O. Krüger, and P. Jernstedt. Tiflis, 1925–35. At present 5 vols.

P. Ryl. = *Catalogue of the Greek Papyri in the John Rylands Library, Manchester*, by A. S. Hunt, J. de M. Johnson, V. Martin, and C. H. Roberts. Manchester, 1911–38. At present 3 vols.

P.S.A. Athen. = *Papyri Societatis Archaeologicae Atheniensis*, by G. A. Petropoulos. Athens, 1939. [The commentaries, &c., are in modern Greek.]

P.S.I. = *Papiri greci e latini* (Pubblicazioni della Società Italiana per la ricerca dei Papiri greci e latini in Egitto), by G. Vitelli, M. Norsa, and others. Florence, 1912 ff. The latest issue is fasc. 1 of vol. xii.

P. Sitol. = *Sitologen-Papyri aus dem Berliner Museum*, by K. Thunell. Uppsala, 1924.

P. Strassb. = *Griechische Papyrus der Kaiserlichen Universitäts- und Landesbibliothek zu Strassburg*, by F. Preisigke. Leipzig, 1912, 1920. 2 vols. [The series was continued by P. Collomp (killed by the Germans during the recent war) and his pupils in *Bull. Fac. Lettr. Strasb.* xiv (1935)–xvii (1939).]

P. Tebt. = *The Tebtunis Papyri*, by B. P. Grenfell, A. S. Hunt, J. G. Smyly, E. J. Goodspeed, and C. C. Edgar. London, 1902–38. 3 vols. (the last in two parts).

P. Thead. = *Papyrus de Théadelphie*, by P. Jouguet. Paris, 1911.

P. Tor. = 'Papyri graeci R. Musei Aegyptii Taurinensis', in *Mem. R. Accad. Torino*, xxxi, 1826, 9–188, xxxiii, 1827, 1–80, by A. Peyron.

P. Ups. 8 = *Der Fluch des Christen Sabinus, Papyrus Upsaliensis 8*, by G. Björck. Uppsala, 1938.

P. Vars. = *Papyri Varsovienses*, by G. Manteuffel. Warsaw, 1935.

P. Vat. gr. 11 = P. Marmarica.

P. Vindob. Boswinkel = *Einige Wiener Papyri* (Papyrologica Lugduno-Batava, ii), by E. Boswinkel. Leyden, 1942.

P. Warren = *The Warren Papyri* (Pap. Lugd.-Bat. i), by M. David, B. A. van Groningen, and J. C. van Oven. Leyden, 1941.

P. Würzb. = *Mitteilungen aus der Würzburger Papyrussammlung*, by U. Wilcken. Berlin, 1934.

SB. See Note 11 to Chap. I.

Stud. Pal. = C. Wessely, *Studien zur Palaeographie und Papyruskunde*. [A periodical publication, issued irregularly and miscellaneous in character.]

UPZ. See Wilcken (U.), under C below.

W. Chrest. = Wilcken, *Chrestomathie*.

B. *Ostraca*

O. Brüss.-Berl. = *Ostraka aus Brüssel und Berlin*, by P. Viereck. Berlin–Leipzig, 1922.

O. Meyer. See **P. Meyer,** under A above.

O. Mich. = *Greek Ostraca in the University of Michigan Collection*, by L. Amundsen. Ann Arbor, 1935.

O. Osl. = *Ostraca Osloënsia*, by L. Amundsen. Oslo, 1933.

O. Pr. Joachim = *Die Prinz-Joachim-Ostraka*, by F. Preisigke and W. Spiegelberg. Strassburg, 1914.

O. Strassb. = *Griechische und griechisch-demotische Ostraka der Universitäts- und Landesbibliothek zu Strassburg im Elsass*, by P. Viereck. Berlin, 1923.

O. Tait = *Greek Ostraca in the Bodleian Library at Oxford and various other Collections*, by J. G. Tait. London, 1930. Only vol. i published at present.

O. Theb. = *Theban Ostraca*. London–Oxford, 1913. [Ostraca in Hieratic, Demotic, Greek, and Coptic. The Greek ostraca edited by J. G. Milne.]

O. Wilb. = *Les Ostraca grecs de la collection Charles-Edwin Wilbour au Musée de Brooklyn*, by C. Préaux. New York, 1935.
W.O. = *Griechische Ostraka aus Aegypten und Nubien*, by U. Wilcken. Leipzig–Berlin, 1899. 2 vols.
Wadi Sarga = *Wadi Sarga: Coptic and Greek Texts*, by W. E. Crum and H. I. Bell. [Papyri and ostraca, in Coptic and Greek. The Greek texts edited by H. I. Bell.]

C. Special Collections of Papyrus Texts

DÖLLSTÄDT (W.), *Griechische Papyrusprivatbriefe in gebildeter Sprache aus den ersten vier Jahrhunderten nach Christus*. Borna–Leipzig, 1934. [A doctoral dissertation at Weimar.]
GHEDINI (G.), *Lettere Cristiane dai papiri greci del III e IV secolo*. Milan, 1923.
LIETZMANN (H.), *Griechische Papyri*. Bonn, 1910 (Kleine Texte für theologische und philologische Vorlesungen und Übungen, 14). [A small selection of representative texts, chiefly letters.]
MEYER (P. M.), *Juristische Papyri*. Berlin, 1920. [A valuable collection of texts illustrating the law of Graeco-Roman Egypt, with elaborate commentaries.]
OLSSON (B.), *Papyrusbriefe aus der frühesten Römerzeit*. Uppsala, 1925.
PREISENDANZ (K.), *Papyri Graecae Magicae*. Leipzig–Berlin, 1928, 1931. 2 vols. [**P.G.M.**]
WILCKEN (U.), *Urkunden der Ptolemäerzeit (ältere Funde)*. Berlin–Leipzig, 1927, &c. [**UPZ.**]
WITKOWSKI (S.), *Epistulae privatae graecae quae in papyris aetatis Lagidarum servantur*. Leipzig, 1906 (2nd edition, 1911).
ZIEBARTH (E.), *Aus der antiken Schule*. Bonn, 1913 (*Kleine Texte*, 65). [A collection of texts from papyri, tablets, and ostraca illustrating school education in Egypt.]
(See also under 'General' above and David–van Groningen, *Papyrological Primer*, under 1.)

3. WORKS ON PALAEOGRAPHY AND DIPLOMATIC

GARDTHAUSEN (V.), *Griechische Palaeographie*; 2nd edition, 2 vols. Leipzig, 1911–13. [A comprehensive work on Greek Palaeography, but including the papyrus period.]
KENYON (F. G.), *The Palaeography of Greek Papyri*. Oxford, 1899. [Now largely out of date but still useful.]

160   *Bibliography*

SCHUBART (W.), *Papyri Graecae Berolinenses*. Bonn, 1911. [A collection of facsimiles, with transcripts, &c.]

SCHUBART (W.), *Griechische Palaeographie*. Munich, 1925. [General work on Greek palaeography, with special attention to papyri.]

THOMPSON (Sir E. Maunde), *An Introduction to Greek and Latin Palaeography*. Oxford, 1912. [A general work on palaeography, but with much information on papyri.]

VAN HOESEN (H. B.), *Roman Cursive Writing*. Princeton, 1915.

KENYON (Sir F. G.), *Books and Readers in Ancient Greece and Rome*. Oxford, 1932.

BIRT (Th.), *Das antike Buchwesen*. Berlin, 1882.

SCHUBART (W.), *Das Buch bei den Griechen und Römern*. Berlin–Leipzig, 1921.   [1934.

LEWIS (N.), *L'Industrie du Papyrus dans l'Égypte Gréco-Romaine*. Paris,

4. *Grammar and Lexicography*

MAYSER (E.), *Grammatik der griechischen Papyri aus der Ptolemäerzeit*. Leipzig, 1906, 1926; rev. ed., in 6 or 7[1] vols.; various dates.

PALMER (L. R.), *A Grammar of the Post-Ptolemaic Papyri*. London, 1946.

KAPSOMENAKIS (S. G.), *Voruntersuchungen zu einer Grammatik der Papyri der nachchristlichen Zeit*. Munich, 1938.

WB. = Preisigke–Kiessling, *Wörterbuch*. See note 9 to Chap. I.

Namenbuch. See note 10 ibid.

GRADENWITZ (O.), *Konträrindex*. See note 13 ibid.

MOULTON (J. H.) and MILLIGAN (G.), *The Vocabulary of the Greek Testament*. London, 1930. [Illustrating New Testament Greek from the language of the papyri.]

LIDDELL (H. G.) and SCOTT (R.), *A Greek-English Lexicon*, New Edition, edited by H. Stuart Jones and R. McKenzie. Oxford, completed 1940. [This latest edition of the famous work makes constant use of the papyrus evidence.]

See also Meecham's *Light from Ancient Letters*, above, 'General'.

5. *Some Works of Reference*

[Monographs on various special subjects and limited periods

---

[1] The volumes of this edition were not issued in the order of the work itself; the sixth to be issued, in 1938, was Vol. I, part 2, after the author's death. Part 1 of this volume remained in manuscript but publication of it, under the editorship of H. Widmann, was then promised. Whether this has appeared I do not know.

are mentioned in the notes and bibliographies to single chapters. Here are mentioned a few useful works which cover the whole Graeco-Roman period. They are arranged by subjects.]

TAUBENSCHLAG (R.), *The Law of Greco-Roman Egypt in the Light of the Papyri*. New York, 1944. (See also Mitteis, *Grundzüge*, above, under 1, and Meyer's *Juristische Papyri*, above, under 2, C.)

SEGRÈ (A.), *Metrologia e circolazione monetaria degli antichi*. Bologna, 1928.

SCHNABEL (M.), *Die Landwirtschaft im hellenistischen Ägypten*, vol. i. Munich, 1925.

OTTO (W.), *Priester und Tempel im hellenistischen Ägypten*. Leipzig–Berlin, 1905–8. [1922–5.

HOPFNER (Th.), *Fontes Historiae Religionis Aegyptiacae*. Bonn,

CHAPTER II

BEVAN (B.), *A History of Egypt under the Ptolemaic Dynasty*. London, 1927.

WILCKEN (U.), *Alexander the Great*. Transl. by G. C. Richards. London, 1932.

JOUGUET (P.), *L'Impérialisme macédonien et l'hellénisation de l'Orient*. Paris, 1926.

TARN (W. W.), *Hellenistic Civilisation*. 2nd ed. London, 1930. Chapter V, 'Egypt'.

ROSTOVTZEFF (M.), *The Social and Economic History of the Hellenistic World*. 3 vols. Oxford, 1941. Chapters on Egypt.

ROSTOVTZEFF (M.), 'Ptolemaic Egypt', in *Cambridge Ancient History*, vii, pp. 109–54.

KÖRTE (A.), *Hellenistic Poetry*. Translated by J. Hammer and M. Hadas. New York, 1929.

PRÉAUX (Claire), *L'Économie royale des Lagides*. Brussels, 1939.

LESQUIER (J.), *Les Institutions militaires de l'Égypte sous les Lagides*. Paris, 1911.

See also, as with following chapters, the works cited in the notes above.

CHAPTER III

MILNE (J. G.), *A History of Egypt under Roman Rule*. London, Methuen. 3rd edition, 1924.

BELL (H. I.), 'Egypt under the Early Principate', *Cambridge Ancient History*, vol. x, chap. x; 'Egypt', ibid., vol. xi, ch. xvi. 1.

162   *Bibliography*

MILNE (J. G.), 'The Ruin of Egypt by Roman Mismanagement', in *Journ. of Rom. Studies*, xvii, 1927, pp. 1–13.

ROSTOVTZEFF (M.), 'The Roman Exploitation of Egypt in the First Century A.D.', in *Journ. of Econ. and Business Hist.* i, 1929, pp. 337–64.

JOUGUET (P.), *La Domination romaine en Égypte aux deux premiers siècles après Jésus-Christ.* Alexandria, Soc. Roy. d'Archéol., 1947.

BELL (H. I.), 'Roman Egypt from Augustus to Diocletian', in *Chron. d'Égypte*, xiii, 1938, pp. 347–63.

ROSTOVTZEFF (M.), *The Social and Economic History of the Roman Empire.* Oxford, Clarendon Press, 1926. [The work was revised for the translations into German (1930) and Italian, and those who can read the latter would be well advised to use the Italian, *Storia economica e sociale dell' impero romano*, Florence, 'La Nuova Italia' Editrice, 1933, which is in effect a third edition.]

JOHNSON (A. C.), *Roman Egypt*, being vol. ii of *An Economic Survey of Ancient Rome.* Baltimore, Johns Hopkins Press, 1936.

JOUGUET (P.), *La Vie municipale dans l'Égypte romaine*, Paris, Fontemoing, 1911.

WALLACE (S. L.), *Taxation in Egypt from Augustus to Diocletian.* Princeton University Press, 1938.

LESQUIER (J.), *L'Armée romaine d'Égypte d'Auguste à Dioclétien*, Cairo, Inst. français d'arch. orientale, 1918.

CHAPTER IV

MILNE (J. G.), *A History of Egypt under Roman Rule.* London, Methuen. 3rd edition, 1924.

GELZER (M.), *Studien zur byzantinischen Verwaltung Ägyptens* (Leipziger Historische Abhandlungen, Heft xiii). Leipzig, 1909.

ROUILLARD (Germaine), *L'Administration civile de l'Égypte byzantine.* 2nd edition, Paris, 1928.

MASPERO (J.), *Organisation milit. de l'Égypte byzantine.* Paris, 1912.

MASPERO (J.), *Histoire des Patriarches d'Alexandrie.* Paris, 1923.

HARDY (E. R.), *The Large Estates of Byzantine Egypt.* New York, 1931.

BELL (H. I.), 'The Byzantine Servile State in Egypt', in *Journ. Eg. Arch.* iv, 1917, pp. 86–106; 'The Decay of a Civilization', ibid. x, 1924, pp. 207–16; 'Egypt and the Byzantine Empire', in *The Legacy of Egypt*, chap. xiii (pp. 332–47).

SEGRÈ (A.), 'The Byzantine Colonate', in *Traditio*, v, 1947, pp. 103–33.

INDEX

(Only such names, &c., in the notes are indexed as do not occur elsewhere or could not be found in that context by references to the text. Purely bibliographical citations are not indexed.)

166   *Index*

High Priest, of Egypt, 68; of *mêtropoleis*, 72.
Hilarianus, procurator, 145.
Hogarth, D. G., 16.
Homer, 13, 14, 54, 61, 81, 82, 128.
Hôrapollôn, professor of philosophy at Alexandria, 149.
Hôrus (Harpocrates), 40.
Hunt, A. S., 16, 17, 19.
Hypatia, 112, 115.
Hyperides, papyri of, 14, 16.
Hypomnêmatographos, 72.
Hypsicratês, 81.
Idios Logos, 21, 68, 76, 78, 141.
Illiteracy, 82.
Indians in Egypt, 53.
Indictio, indiction, 99, 102–3.
Inflation, monetary, 59, 94.
Inscriptions, 10, 22–3.
Isidôros, landowner at Theadelphia, 149.
Isis, 40, 114.
Issus, Battle of, 28.
Iugatio, iugum, 99, 100, 117.
Jacobites, 116.
Jerusalem, capture of, by the Persians, 129; Mosque of, 134.
Jews of Alexandria, 52, 54, 70, 89–90, 112, 133.
John, St., Gospel of, 18, 86, 88.
Johnson, John, 18.
Juridicus, 68, 141.
Justinian, 102, 121, 125, 133.
Juvenal, 127.
Karanis, in the Fayyûm, 80, 149.
Katochê, 108.
Katoikoi, 70.
Klêroi (allotments), 35, 36, 45, 60.
Klêrouchoi, see Cleruchs.
Koinê (international Greek), 36.
Koinodikion, 43.
Kollêmata of papyrus, 7.
Land policy, 44–7, 73–4.
Laokritai, court of, 43.
Latin, use of, in Egypt, 102–3, 127.
Law in Egypt, 42–3, Roman, 93.
Leo I, 120.
Library of Alexandria, 53–4.
Licinius, 105.
Liturgies and liturgical system, 79, 84–5, 92–4, 137, 149.

Logia (Sayings) of Jesus, 16, 17.
Louis, St., of France, 3.
Macedonians, position of, 34, 35, 52.
Magas, brother of Ptolemy IV, 140.
Magistrates and magistracies, municipal, 71–2, 79, 84–5, 92–4.
Mahomet, 130–1.
Manetho, 37.
Mareôtis, Lake, 30, 51.
Mark, St., alleged foundation by, of Alexandrian Church, 86.
Martyrs, Era of the, 104.
Maspero, Jean, 115.
Maurice, Emperor, 128.
Maxentius, 104.
Maximian, Emperor, 100.
Mazacês, satrap of Egypt, 29.
Melitians, 108.
Melkites, 116.
Memphis, 29, 30, 33, 39, 67.
Menander, 81, 128.
Mendesian nome, 11.
Mêtropoleis, 69, 91–4, 101, 126–7.
Metropolites, privileged, 70–1.
Michigan, University of, 80–1.
Milan, Edict of, 105.
Milvian Bridge, Battle of the, 105.
Minucius Timinianus, 145.
Mithras, 40.
Moeris, Lake of, 3.
Monasticism, 108–14, 127.
Monophysite heresy, 114–16, 127.
Monopolies, state, 48–50, 135.
Monotheism and polytheism, 107.
Monothelite heresy, 131.
Monsoon, discovery of, 53, 75.
Municipal government, 72, 101, 126–7.
Museum, at Alexandria, 53, 90.
Musical entertainments, 84.
Nationalism, Egyptian, 37, 68, 113–14.
Natron monopoly, 49.
Naucratis, 34, 42.
Nero, 77, 78, 89.
Nestôrius, 115.
Nicêtas, 4, 129.
Nock, A. D., 147.
Nomarch, 43.